Out of the SHADOWS

Editors

Sandra Joy, Pam Garfoot and

Alison Ferguson

Out of the SHADOWS

Best short stories and poetry
Alice Sinclair Memorial Writing Competition
2022

Editors

Sandra Joy, Pam Garfoot and

Alison Ferguson

Lake Macquarie Branch of the
Fellowship of Australian Writers

Out of the Shadows: *Best short stories and poetry, Alice Sinclair Memorial Writing Competition 2022.*

First published in March 2023 by the Lake Macquarie Branch of the Fellowship of Australian Writers, NSW.
www.lakemacfaw2.wordpress.com

A catalogue record for this work is available from the National Library of Australia

Cover design by Scott Mair
Illustrations by Pam Garfoot and Bethany Wooden
Type: Palatino Linotype

Lake Macquarie FAW titles:
978-1-876409-63-0 Beneath the Surface (paperback)
978-1-876409-49-4 Beneath the Surface (e-book)
978-0-909497-05-7 Beneath the Surface (large print)
978-0-909497-90-3 Out of the Shadows (paperback)
978-1-876409-05-0 Out of the Shadows (e-book)

Contents

Section 3: NOT SO OLD …

Section 4: A GROWING THING …

Section 5: BEATING BACK THE BLOWS …

Introduction

There's something inspirational about writing to a theme, especially one as tantalising as 'Out of the Shadows'. The entrants in our 2022 Alice Sinclair Memorial Writing Competition (lovingly shortened to the Alice Sinclair competition) warmed to their task and gave us a huge array of interpretations of the shadows theme in their poems and short stories. The best of these are represented here in this anthology, the second produced by the Lake Macquarie Branch of the Fellowship of Australian Writers, NSW. The group's first anthology, *Beneath the Surface*, was published in 2020.

The biennial Alice Sinclair competition began in 2004 as a tribute to the late Alice Sinclair who had been a significant driving force in the establishment of the branch. When first held, the competition was purely 'in house' with only a handful of entrants, but with the passing years its scope and the number of entrants has grown.

Now the competition is a truly 'open' competition attracting entrants from across Australia. This year we received a record number of entries: 208 entries in all (88 in the Poetry Category and 120 in the Short Story Category). And, of course, they were judged entirely 'blindly' by Magdalena Ball and Jenny Blackford.

Magdalena is a novelist, poet, reviewer, interviewer, and the editor of *Compulsive Reader*. She has been widely published in literary journals, anthologies, and is the author of several books of poetry and fiction.

Jenny writes poems and stories for people of all ages, usually with a tinge of myth and legend, ancient history, science, or deep time. Over 40 of her short stories and over 150 of her poems have appeared in Australian and international anthologies and journals.

The large pool of entrants meant that we were asking for a mammoth effort from our judges. However, the judges have selected for us a great shortlist of pieces spanning a wide variety of writing styles and techniques. The first prize winners, Janice Williams with 'Boy with a Trumpet' and Marc Cannella with 'Distant Fires', are certainly impressive and must be congratulated. Congratulations must also go to the other place getters, Kathryn Fry, Ned Stephenson, Gideon McDonald, Edith Speers and Roslyn Varley.

We must thank the judges for their hard work, and also the competition convenors, Sandra Boyd and Olga Korlevic. George Graves, the group's treasurer, has helped us steer a steady financial course. Our beautiful cover design has once again been created by Scott Mair, and the black and white illustrations throughout the anthology have been done by Bethany Wooden and Pam Garfoot.

We hope the fine poems and stories included in *Out of the Shadows* provide much enjoyment to those who read them.

Sandra Boyd, Olga Korlevic, Pam Garfoot,
Alison Ferguson, Bethany Wooden
Anthology Editorial Committee

Judges' Foreword

With eighty-eight poems and one hundred and twenty stories, the competition was pretty intense. The kinds of things we were looking for were original imagery, a powerful premise, a good arc, strong narration or rhythms.

All judging is subjective to an extent, and anyone who didn't make the anthology should keep that in mind. The judges have specific tastes and although we applied consistent criteria and tried to be as objective as possible, there were stories and poems that had us returning to them for reasons that were subtle and sometimes went beyond the judging criteria.

Every entrant is to be congratulated for taking the time to pull together a submission and edit it to be their best work. It's often this editing process that makes all the difference between a good piece of work and a great one.

The thirty pieces of shortlisted work that made it into the anthology, really came down to the elements of good writing working: powerful imagery, strong rhythms, original concepts, and something hard to pin down – a kind of beauty combined with honesty that kept us thinking about the work. These pieces were generally the more ambitious stories and poems that tried to tackle something that can't be said easily, which is why it's such good fodder for creative writing.

In terms of stories, they were chosen for their compelling characters and page-turning plots, with prose of Marc Cannella in 'Distant Fires' leading you into a dazzling metafictional echo of Jane Austen, mixed with a touch of H.G. Wells. Prepare for a mysterious and wonderful ride through time.

Ned Stephenson's 'Son of Prometheus' seems, initially, to be a simple story of a woman who takes dust to a local potter, to have it incorporated into three special bowls. The story leads the unsuspecting reader to a stunningly understated ending.

Edith Speers' 'The Flying Fortuna Sister' is, from its first sentence onwards, an amazingly different story with simple, stylised prose. A fabulously different child is forced into conformity, with the best of intentions. As she grows older, she attempts to be 'normal' for other people's sake. The ending is almost predictable, but totally charming.

In Roslyn Varley's 'Ghosts', a woman preparing to leave her family's old farmstead finds herself playing cards and drinking whisky with the ghost of her dryly funny mother, who reveals a clue to a devastating secret.

For the poems, Gideon McDonald's third placed 'Between the Speckled Lights' made good use of the page and created a powerful soundscape bouncing off the Calvino epigraph, that worked like ekphrasis for this piece, adding resonance. The play between darkness and light, and the repetition of "brown dirt, red dirt, yellow dirt, I" worked perfectly and sounded even better recited, which the poem encouraged. This poem is an excellent example of how to use sound to create meaning in a poem.

There were a number of garden poems and many of them were good, but what set the second place poem, Kathryn Fry's 'The Old Sand Mining Site', apart was the way it combined its soft, gentle imagery with a walking rhythm that set the pace perfectly for its invocation and the more subtle but inherent message around the importance of paying attention and the way that the natural world has stories for all of us.

Janice Williams' 'Boy with a Trumpet' hit all of the criteria for good poetry including the intangible 'wow' that changes reality. On the surface this is simply a poem about a young boy playing a trumpet on Anzac Day 2020, but so much happens here, and with such delicate capability. The repetition of "Come home, come home" provides a refrain which picks up the sound of the trumpet when it blows and is filled with a sense of nostalgia bringing the past into the present in a way that good poetry can do when it's working at this high level. How lovely and sad this poem is and yet it also contains within its perfectly structured rhythms a sense of renewal as the sun comes up (a "silver sunlight-thread"), the trumpet blower himself representing the future as the music does its magic.

Congratulations to all of the winners, the shortlisted writers included in this lovely anthology and indeed everyone who submitted.

Jenny Blackford
Magdalena Ball

SECTION 1

ONCE UPON A TIME ...

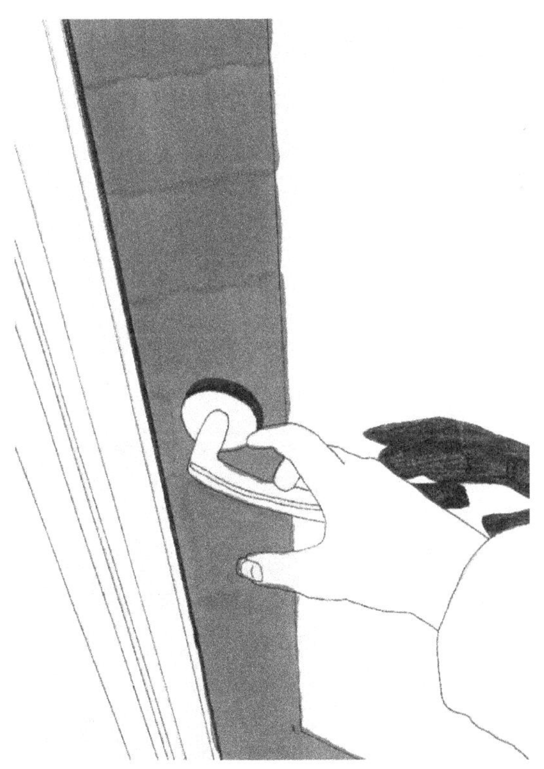

The Flying Fortuna Sister

Edith Speers

This story was awarded a *Highly Commended* in the short story category of the Alice Sinclair Memorial Writing Competition.

Once upon a time there was a person who was not normal. This person was born in the normal way to a normal family so for a while no one noticed that she was different. She was carried inside her mother for about nine months. This was normal. The mother was worried all the time and the baby knew it. This was also quite normal. The mother worried because she had carried two other babies at different times in her life and both of these babies had something wrong with them.

The first baby had so many things wrong with her that she died very soon after she was born. The mother never talked about her ever again. This was fairly normal. The second baby had something wrong with one foot. It did not hurt him but it was not normal. The mother and the father gave him to some doctors who kept him in a hospital for a long time and cut open his foot and did things to it to try to make it normal. Then his foot hurt. He wore a special shoe all his life because his foot hurt and also the shoe helped him to look more like other people. The boy did not like to be hurt and he did not like to wear a special shoe but he wanted to look like other people. This was normal.

The third baby looked alright at first. She had nothing wrong with her. Her parents named her Fortuna which means luck because they felt lucky to have a nice normal baby. But one day very soon after Fortuna was born the mother went into the bedroom where the baby was sleeping in her cot. The baby was still sleeping in the cot but she was not sleeping on the cot. She was floating about halfway up the height of the bars on the cot. This was not normal.

The mother screamed and ran to get the father. The scream woke the baby who knew something was wrong and worried about it. By the time her parents came back to the bedroom she was lying on the mattress of the cot. She was awake and she was crying.

"What's wrong with her?" asked the father.

"I don't know," said the mother. The mother did not tell the father that she saw the baby floating. She pretended it never happened.

The father said, "There's nothing wrong with her. All babies cry. You are worrying too much."

The mother agreed. The mother and father smiled at each other because all of this was very normal.

But a few days later the father walked into the bedroom where the baby was sleeping in her cot but not on her cot. He did not scream. He stood there and stared at her. He walked closer very quietly to have a better look. He was still standing there when the mother walked in. She was talking as she walked in but then she stopped talking. The father turned and looked at her. She looked away from him but when she looked away from him she could not stop herself from looking at the baby again. Then she hunched up her shoulders and bowed her head. She covered her face with her two hands and began to cry.

"It's not my fault," she cried. "Why me?"

The father went and hugged the mother.

"It's not your fault," he said.

The mother cried and the father hugged her. After a while they both turned and looked at the baby again. She was lying on the mattress of her cot. She was awake but she was not crying. She was watching them and she looked worried.

"She looks so normal," said the mother. "Maybe, maybe it didn't happen."

"It happened," said the father. "But there's nothing wrong with her, nothing that can't be fixed. I'm sure of it."

"Maybe she'll grow out of it," the mother said.

During the times when she was awake the baby knew that her parents were worried about her. She did not float. But when she went to sleep she forgot about the worrying. Then she floated. So her parents tied her down at night and also during her daytime sleeping. They used straps with buckles to tie her down onto the mattress of the cot. Then they covered Fortuna and the straps and buckles with a blanket so that no one else would know about it.

When they took Fortuna and her brother to visit other people then the parents worried about her a lot. Fortuna knew about this and she did not want to float but she felt so happy not to be tied down when she slept that she knew she was going to float as soon as she fell asleep. So, before she fell asleep at the place they were visiting, Fortuna did some thinking. She thought about the first baby. Did she want to be a baby whose name was never spoken? No, she did not. She thought about the second baby. Did she want to be taken away by doctors who cut into her body and made her feel hurt for the rest of her life? No, she did not. Fortuna took these two worries with her into her sleep. She did not float.

The parents were very glad. At home they also saw that Fortuna did not float during her daytime sleeping.

"Maybe she's grown out of it," said the mother.

The father smiled and said, "I told you there was nothing wrong with her."

But they kept tying her down at night-time anyway, just in case. Slowly they stopped worrying. Then they did not use the straps anymore. Finally, they threw away the straps.

Fortuna was so happy about this that one night she woke up in the dark when she was floating. She was awake but she did not stop floating. She was almost up to the ceiling and she was not scared. She liked it.

Then she thought about her parents and she sank about halfway down to the mattress again. Then she thought about the first baby and sank some more and she thought about the second baby and sank some more. She thought about the straps and sank far enough down that she was inside the cot but not on the cot. What else was there to worry about? If she could not think of something to worry about then she was in trouble. As she worried about not finding something to worry about, Fortuna felt herself land with a soft thud on the mattress. She jumped a bit because it was a surprise. Then she fell asleep.

As Fortuna grew up she forgot about the floating but she did not forget about the worrying. Often she woke up in bed as she felt herself land with a soft thud. She jumped a bit because it was a surprise. Then she fell asleep. That was in the night-time.

In the daytime Fortuna was a happy child. Sometimes she was so happy she almost floated. But then it happened that she worried about something and she felt heavy again. She worried that the bogeyman was hiding under her bed. As soon as she turned off the bedroom light she ran and jumped into bed. That stopped him from grabbing her by the ankles as she climbed into bed. The trouble was that she liked the running and jumping so much that it made her laugh. Then she worried about having fun with the bogeyman. It wasn't normal.

In the morning she shook out each of her shoes before she put her foot into it. This was to make sure that the bogeyman wasn't hiding in the toe of her shoe waiting to bite her toe like a spider. But it was so funny to think about a bogeyman who was big enough to eat her alive but also small enough to fit in the toe of her shoe that thinking about it made her laugh. Then she worried about the things she thought.

Fortuna knew that she thought about a lot of strange things that no one else ever thought about. Strange things came into her mind all the time. She knew she wasn't normal. For a very long time this was her most important worry and the only one that always kept her from floating.

Fortuna grew up and worried about everything that normal people worry about. She worried about school and friends and enemies. She worried about getting a job and making money. She worried about falling in love and getting married and having children. Whenever she was almost perfectly happy then another worry came along.

But finally everything happened very close together. All in a very short time of a few years every worry she had ever worried about all came true. Almost every bad thing that was possible happened to her all in a very short time of a few years. First her father died. Then she fell in love and got married and moved to a far city where she had no friends. Her brother got religious and wouldn't write to her anymore because she was not religious. Then her mother died. Then she found out she didn't want to have any babies. Next, she fell out of love and got divorced. After that she lost her job and was very poor. She cried and cried. For years it seemed like all she did was cry and feel hurt inside and there was no one left in the world to speak her name.

One night she went to bed feeling very tired. She was too tired to cry and too tired to think about her worries. She just slept. In the morning when she woke up she was floating between the bed and the ceiling. She was awake but she did not stop floating. She was almost up to the ceiling and she was not scared. She liked it.

"I knew it," she said out loud. "I knew I wasn't normal."

But she didn't worry about it. She spent the whole day floating around the house and thinking about things. She worried just enough about burning the toast to keep from bumping into the ceiling and she worried just enough about bumping into the ceiling to keep her down where she could grab the toast before it burnt. Mostly she spent the day thinking about what she wanted to do now that she wasn't worried about not being normal.

Fortuna was very sure of two things. First of all, she did not want anyone else to know that she could float. She was pretty sure that this worry was strong enough to keep her feet on the ground when she was with other people. Secondly, she wanted to find out if there were other people who could float. This meant she must travel to different parts of the world and she must try to meet people who were also looking for other people who could float. This meant she must have a job where she could travel and make a lot of money and meet strange people. She went to work for a circus.

She worked as a ticket seller for a while. But soon she learned how to be a bareback rider. Then she learned how to be a tightrope walker and finally she learned how to be a trapeze artist. Even though she knew how to float it was not easy to learn these things. She worked hard. She worried just enough to look normal as she learned these things. When she was learning to be a trapeze artist she was so happy to be free in the air that she sometimes forgot to worry if the other artists would find out she could float. A couple of times they almost found out. A couple of times it also happened that it was a good thing she knew how to float even if people almost found out.

One time her partner did not grab her by the wrists at the right time and everyone knew she must fall. But she did not fall. Somehow, she grabbed his wrists. People looked at her in a strange way for a while after that. Another time she was working with another artist very high out of doors and they had no net beneath them. As she let go of her trapeze and flew out to where her partner must catch her by the wrists, his trapeze broke. They both fell. But somehow Fortuna fell sideways and bumped into him and they both fell on top of a canvas tent. People ran and helped them to get up from where the tent had fallen down beneath them. Everyone agreed they were very lucky to be alive. People looked at Fortuna in a strange way for a long while after that.

Then she knew she must work alone. She left that circus and went to another country and another circus. She went and talked to the big boss of the circus about getting a job. It was a very famous circus. It paid a lot of money and it went all over the world. She explained to the man who was the boss that she worked alone.

"But what about your sister?" asked the man.

Fortuna thought about the first baby and she said, "I have a sister but she's not in the act."

"But you're called the Flying Fortuna Sisters," said the man.

"No," said Fortuna. "I'm called the Flying Fortuna Sister. There's just one of me. At the moment there's just one of me." She smiled.

"That's a strange name for an act," said the man.

Fortuna shrugged and said, "That's the name of my act."

"Okay, sister," said the man. "I've heard you're good. You can call yourself anything you like so long as the people will pay to see you."

"No worries," said Fortuna.

Miasma

Pippa Kay

Infection drifts
and rises with the sun.

She comes from deep in the forest,
like a child who has played too long
in the gloom.
Her skirt is too long.
It folds about her feet.
She must lift it,
step out of the foetid muck
that covers the forest floor
that stains her skirt and feet.

The stench is suffocating
— a winding sheet.
It wafts through the village
as she approaches.
Villagers fear bad air
close their doors against contagion.

Yet, she glides like a ghost
through laneways and back alleys.
Villagers swear
her feet do not touch the ground.

Hold your breath as she passes.
She's not human, they warn.
She decays,
like the litter on the forest floor
— becomes the miasma.

Let There be a Firmament

Kate Maxwell

Firm footed over centuries; palms pressed to hips
or leaning heavily on hoe to take another thirsty swig
   we took pause to peer at birds soaring into blue

tracked the fading curve of wings to brilliant blur
of eyesight's limits and wondered what they already
knew. Secrets of the birds stayed hidden many years.

Tower building, mountain scaling to mimic higher
views, we scanned seas, cities, plains, yet saw only
flat horizons falling into unexplained extinction.

Knew nothing beyond our selves, so gave ourselves
            forever: claimed earth a holy tabernacle
between heaven and hell, the sun and seasons

merely whims of gods or demons. So much easier
to grasp such deified benevolence or sanction
than the yet uncharted, and unwanted truth;

            that earth just spins its furtive sliding roll
beneath our very feet. Myths and creeds made
fillers for our minds' black holes: empty spaces

shimmering with storied stars of hunters, lions
and bears, all pitched in silver fight or flight
above our tiny heads. Fantastically, in ancient India

sky gazers declared our globe secured on backs
of monstrous elephants which, in turn, stood upon
the back of a colossal turtle forever swimming

a black and waterless ocean. And, even legend's boy
who flew on wings of feathers and wax to search
the vast unknown, found no answers in the inky void

but fell to earth in melting shame of imagination's
limits. Icarus, first space traveller who flew too close
to the sun, just another fiery caution to our astronomical

yearnings. Best to keep faith in accepted lies and frail
absurdities, burn detractors' words and bodies at the stake
those who dare to pose the brittle possibility that we

may not be the centre or reason of all, but simply specks
in a universe of floating specks. Yet, in our science
saturated world, with tested hypotheses, men upon the moon

and planet-sized brains continuing to unmask answers
of the aerial abyss some still claim their comfort
in a dark age disregard of awkward truths, preferring

fiction and alternative facts. I too, will concede
a reverenced terror of the air-sucking beyond
still chills my veins when I stare long into the night.

Mouse Tail

Peter Court

'Twas the night before all souls and all through the house nothing was stirring, except the damn mouse. The children are safe all tucked up in their beds, but the bastard is lurking with talons of dread. I've known of his presence for five or six weeks, the telltale turds and the curdling shrieks. At night when I'm resting he'll sneak under my bed and let loose a howl like a child being bled. I've plied him with cheeses, with stale meats and wraps, but still he's avoided the snap of my traps. Then baits were laid down, they were gut tearing lethal. We still have the mouse but I've murdered our beagle.

So into the garden I venture this time, my serious daughter says, "Whadidya say?"

"I'm sorry dear?"

"You were mumbling something. You always do that when you're really angry."

She says 'weally angwy', as young ones are wont to do. It's so annoying.

"I'm not angry," as I stamp with passion upon the loose soil, leaving a satisfactory imprint. She's right of course, and I hate that too.

"Daddy!"

"Huh? Oh, sorry ..." I withdraw my clumsy boot from the grave earth and gently pat down the loose soil with my shovel leaving Benji, the beagle, to rot in peace.

The mouse ate the last of the wedding cake, the white top tier, now yellowing with age. Only a month ago I was looking at it. I do that sometimes. It's a strange feeling. The old things are things that are old because I look at them alone. They were never old when she was here. And the concrete curb of yellowing icing had crumbled at the corner, a salt damp in its construction. I put aside the glass of wine and the ache in my throat to draw the dispassionate square down from the shelf. As I did so it trembled, as if excited. Or fearful. It is too light. It is hollow. Squinting in through the crumbled corner there is no longer any substance to the wedding cake, just the hard outer crust. And, within, a whole lot of mouse turds.

My son, Robert, is smaller than his size, as if he also has been hollowed in some way. As I place traps, I explain the vermin in our midst. Now he believes the mouse wants to steal his dark chocolate nipples while he sleeps, that he will awake to a bloodied chest, ripped with pain. I try to find bed-time stories in which mice are destroyed and their reign of sneaking deceit is ended. But for some reason children's authors see mice as heroes. These are probably the same people who see only priests and not the paedophiles. Romantic tales of cutesy rodents will not bring sleep, only put a clown's face on the executioner, so I find myself perched on Robert's candy flavoured quilt, rubbing his whispering hair, making it up.

"… and the baby mice, hidden in their nest of stolen wire, heard the distant SNAP as the evil black mouse met his doom."

"But what about the baby mices?"

"… um … oh, well, they realised they were free now to escape the horrible wire nest and ran to the beautiful park where they could live in the happy trees. The End."

The approaching night waits patiently whilst Robert unfurls the story in his head.

"But won't the cats eat them in the park?"

"Well … maybe … but, they're mice. What's better? Fat happy cat or fat happy mouse?"

Again, his eyes are held back in consideration. Then …

"Both?"

"Mice don't eat nipples, Robbo. Go to sleep."

The house is so quiet at night. The gurgle and whisper of the children breathing, the soft reassurance of technology humming along as it does its work, and the air paused, sitting easily, peaceful. And then there is the noise. Hard chalk scraping, screeling on polystyrene. It stops. The 'fridge clicks, hums. Something is grinding at wood, slowly, and then scraping again. A tiny sound, so distant, so small, so powerful. And then not. It is as if my own heart has stopped. The silence is worse. The absence means something hidden. Then it starts again. No, this is worse. The tiny noise. No, the silence, now this is worse. All night. The pillow over my head stinks of my own hair. And sweat. I itch, my scalp crawls at the sound that I can only hear when I don't really try to listen. I sleep for moments but don't rest. The morning brightens only to cast shadows under my eyes and in the mirror I see the man who has been left behind, confused. She has gone and I remain to fear what has happened. She had always felt herself to be too big for her own skin. At times she would slice and pare herself, letting out gathers and gussets of sour worry. It was enough to drive a bloke nuts. Perhaps this is why she is gone.

I didn't really want to bring up these two children by myself. But it became more and more obvious that she sure as hell shouldn't do it. Parenting is an adult task. Grown ups. People who can find the solution, protect and defend. As I slide another trap, this one beneath the sanctified white coolness of the 'fridge, I feel that surge of protective pride, the rightness of it all. Life is good. Mouse is bad.

Evening is seeking to rest again. The dreamy air is thick with coagulating mist, rendering the surrounding roof tops as a marching phalanx of increasingly vague cardboard cut-outs. Inside the paint and concrete of our home the children are draping toward sleep and I am raw. On my biscuits, my relaxing luxury, there must have been telltale scratches. Tiny, unnoticed, to be thought nothing of, until these cramps and this coiling acid belly have driven everything else from me. Some vile virus he carries, he has left for me to consume and I have innocently swallowed his poison. I try not to alert the children as they busy about with the usual. Teeth are brushed, beds avoided, jokes and jibes are being slung back and forth as they parade about within the house.

In the darkening garden I hang over the variegated leaves of the vines, watching my insides become outside. I vomit quietly, ashamed, whipped. Between heaving spasms I am grateful for this little garden of vine draped fence and the lawn that now holds the rotting dog, and I stare at the green and growing space that she never really appreciated. I wonder how she feels about it now. Quite a home.

He watches me whilst I sleep. I don't need to open my eyes. I can feel him. His tiny little eyes, occult drops of poisonous oil, gaze at me. Watching. From the dark corner beneath the dressing table. I can feel his hate, a snickering razor sharp, blackness transmitted from his tiny, obsidian eyes. He broods, seethes, stares at me as I sleep. Just like she did, her eyes slitted just open so I won't know. I don't need to look but I know. I've felt those surgical eyes piercing, digging, stabbing. Her eyes. His eyes. Whilst I sleep. If only for this, I must rid the house of them.

Toast warmth fills the morning air. Fresh, yeasty butter and soft padding feet from the kitchen. It stinks. I've not rested, merely decided. I don't need a pest exterminator, not a mass killer to eradicate a population. No. It's only the one who is causing this infection. Once he is gone, peace can return. I need a pest executioner. An assassin, a hit-man. Who will rid me of this troublesome rodent? Who can I call? And why is the phone not working?

Now I'm angry. Unrested, unsettled and angry. As I tumble about in the roof space, carefully stepping on the rough wooden beams of the ceiling I realise how angry. My skull fills with a rhyming pattern, a mental self-medication, muttering as I shuffle the bricks to fit the pattern, to solve the dark deepening gnaw.

The phone has been bitter, a terrible matter,

so from inside the roof arose such a clatter...

I can't find where the mouse has torn through the phone lines. Smart little bastard. I jump from the roof cavity and land in a pool of my own seething. Two crumb bedecked faces look up at me from their pyjamas.

"WHAT?!" and they are fearful. They have seen this before.

"Oh daddy ... no," she lisps from behind a mouthful of warm toast.

Oh yes, the little one must die.

For days, weeks, I answered her friends. At the door, on the phone. "She's gone" – "I don't know" – "You know how she was" – "She didn't say". And soon enough they just stopped calling, faded away. She was gone. And so she is and always shall be.

The mouse trap is a beautiful creation. Simplicity. Easy and deadly. And more than execution, it is also exoneration. If not for the mouse's own greed, the very thing that leads it to the trap, it would surely survive. So not only does it die in a flashing moment of snapping horror, at that same moment it deserves to die for its selfishness and insatiable lust. A storehouse of kinetic violence unleashed by the beast's own hunger. Bringing down death upon its own head. This trap I place beneath the sofa in the sunroom where once we had sat, she and I, before she had turned within herself for value, back when I had been her friend and lover. We would sit here in the sun and ponder the beauty of ourselves. Then, as if sterilised by too much sun, she had drained of that simple joy, that heart of warmth. The wax had melted, drained and her joints had simply fallen in, leaving a hollow wreck of the woman I had loved. She could no longer be here. She had to go. Perhaps it is the nature of nature that this is also where the mouse has put himself to death. The steel bar has pounded down upon his glowing neck and crushed the chalk of his spine in a blink. He has gone. The mouse has left now.

A single boot covers the tiny grave. It is a mark of my respect for the passed foe. He was valiant but now he has gone. The bare earth will soon return to lawned peace, like the grave of Benji is beginning to do. And the other one too. Peace has returned again and the gentle warmth of the velvet evening is a soft salve. Peace flows in. Nothing can disturb me now. Except those bloody children! What the hell are they shouting about. Dammit, I'll need to sort them out …

The Great Seal

Ian Reid

Withstanding years of earnest scrutiny,
this painting remains tight-lipped, gives little away.
But its title conjures a world where Kublai Khan

presents to Marco Polo a tablet of gold
imprinted with his great seal and inscribed
with a message vouching for its intrepid envoy.

The seal's ink paste itself, Marco records,
is made of cinnabar, mulberry-red
— much the same colour as this picture's ground.

Thin oblong figures, strands of creamy silk
arranged in rows, box-like, appear to float
on the painted surface, indecipherable.

In the murk behind them there are hints
of limbs that sprawl, as if a body is either
idly receptive or almost falling apart.

Beneath the patterning, something unruly stirs.
Nearly discernible, is that your phantom self
emerging from shadows of a fabled past?

This poem was inspired by a painting by Ben Joel.

Rapunzel and the Awakening

Black Crow Walking

Sequel 1: Two years later.

Rapunzel remembered the day the Prince was thrown from the tower window by the Witch and blinded by brambles at the bottom. She felt the horror of his terrified screams, and her anger rose at the thought of her loss. Rapunzel had looked at the Witch as her mother, who taught her the healing crafts. She had often gone to the secret door with the intent to leave and tried to open it. But a strange sensation came over her as if she had forgotten why she went to the door. Her body became tingly and her mind quite foggy. It often took an hour to shake off the feeling of confusion. After a while, she had forgotten the door existed even though she saw the Witch go through it; in Rapunzel's mind, the Witch seemed to vanish through the wall.

The Witch told her she was with child, which was her punishment for allowing the Prince to take her innocence. Rapunzel felt sick in the mornings as her belly grew. The Witch made up herbal tea that calmed her and stopped the sickness. Rapunzel had never learned the world's ways; she didn't have to; her world was in this tower with her passion for learning alchemy.

Rapunzel often gazed longingly out the window to brush her very long hair so as not to get hair all over the floor of her tower room. She noticed the Witch had collected her hair in an 'EXIT' labelled jar in the apothecary. Once she saw a bird catch her golden hair in mid-air and drag it to the trees. It would have had enough to weave a whole nest with just one strand.

An older man and lady lived next door, and she would catch the woman looking up at the tower and wave at her, but the woman always hid her face in a handkerchief and ran inside. The man spent most of his days in his well-kept garden but never looked at the tower. His old back was bent as if carrying a heavy load, and a strange feeling of sorrow overcame her as she watched him weeding.

Rapunzel bore healthy twin boy babies; to the Witch's delight, one had golden hair, the other black. She called them Sunny and Shadow. Rapunzel longed for a garden for them to play in and looked longingly next door.

Meanwhile:- Nine months earlier, the Prince, with damaged eyes that could barely make out shapes, found the brambles parted to create a pathway out. He expected to find his horse and the forest, but there was hot, dry sand underfoot, a desert! Occasionally, the Prince would hear his horse neighing in the distance and follow the sound, which led him to berry bushes and water holes. A passer-by would leave a loaf of bread and water for him; he wouldn't see them but found the food in his lap when he awoke.

He began to understand kindness.

He remembered stopping at the small cottage next to the tower and asking for directions and water for his horse. He had talked to the couple while his horse drank, and knowing him to be a prince, they told him the story of how their daughter had been taken from them by the Witch next door and locked in the tower. They had hoped he might be able to help somehow.

He had walked around the garden at the back of the house and looked up at the tower. At that precise moment, Rapunzel appeared and began to let down her golden hair outside the window and run her fingers down it to release any knots. Her hair shone like spun gold, and she sang to the birds gathered in the nearby trees.

The Prince remembered a strange feeling in his heart, and an immense joy enveloped his whole being. He had not experienced love before; it was new to him. Strange thoughts of rescue and protection filled his mind. The man appeared beside him and looked up at the tower, saying, "Oh, if only I had not listened to my wife's pregnant cravings, she would still be ours". The Prince saw a tear in the man's eyes and asked what had happened. "I didn't have a garden then, but the Witch did. My wife asked me to bring her food from the Witch's Garden. I did and got caught by the Witch; she only let me live on the provision that I give her our first-born child. I had no choice; she appeared in our bedroom the minute my wife gave birth and took the child. My wife never got over it, and I regret it every day." From that moment, the Prince became obsessed with the woman in the tower.

After two years of wandering in the desert, blinded by his desire for Rapunzel and her hair, he found solace in the desert's silence. She had plaited her hair as a rope the first time she saw him and wrapped it around a pike. He climbed it. He could have cut it off, brought her down the rope and rode her back to his castle. But it was her hair he loved.

He regretted not bringing an army to kill the damn Witch instead of sneaking in when she was gone collecting herbs for secret potions in the woods. Was it better to face her curses than to bear the responsibility of his role as Prince?

He preferred the fairy-tale of the elusive Rapunzel. Not the woman that would bear his sons and live happily, or not, ever after. When he gave it some thought, what would a woman be like who had lived in her locked-up world with no social skills? She hardly fitted as a Prince's wife. He couldn't bring her into this kingdom with two illegitimate children; the shame on his parents! Yet if he could see her one more time, maybe he could set it right.

Rapunzel looked at the bottle with her hair; there was a strange longing in her as she looked at that word, a strong desire to exit. She knew what to do now.

Her training with the Witch had taught her the law of opposites. She gathered the two boys and took the jar down to the bottom of the stairs. There before her was a door; she vaguely remembered it. Before she could think, she flung the bottle at the door, shouted "Entry", grabbed hold of the handle and threw the door open. Before her was a vast desert, she took a tentative step with the boys and began to run.

The Prince heard the sound of running feet and realised Rapunzel was there as she called out to him. She was cradling his head against her bosom, crying tears of joy that dropped into his eyes, breaking the Witch's curse. Those same sweet eyes were looking down on him, and two small boys, looking bewildered, hid behind her skirts. They had never seen a man before.

He shielded the light from his eyes as they hurt, rubbing them till they adjusted. He was aching with possibilities as his sight returned. Looking at Rapunzel, he knew they lived this fantasy together. He saw his potential as a man beyond the role of the Prince, for once.

His faithful horse was grazing not far from him. He stood up and touched her face; he would take her with him. And what of these boys who had his blue eyes? He knelt to inspect them, and they pulled in closer behind Rapunzel's skirt. It would take time, but he was different now, and perhaps, so was she. She had broken away from the Witch's spells and sought her freedom; her love had restored his sight. Somehow, he had grown up and with that came the truth.

Rapunzel looked at him, dressed in rags, looking nothing like the man who had won her heart and felt compassion.

Rapunzel had broken the spell, and they were all free. Her boys would know the truth of love.

Sequel to Rapunzel 2: Two Centuries later, 2022

Rapunzel was late leaving the office this evening; she loved her work. She had little time for social life, and other employees accused her of living in an ivory tower. Her office was on the twenty-sixth floor and overlooked the entire city. She saw herself in the category of a nerd. She had topped her class in biochemistry and was sought after by many companies but wasn't interested in the egocentric world of competition. She was happy on her own and liked to be left alone. She often got to work earlier than necessary and left late to avoid the other workers.

The company she worked for was the head office for England, a worldwide franchise. It was run by a tyrannical woman known unaffectionately as 'the Hag'. She was constantly tossing insults at the staff and cursing under her breath. For some strange reason, she had taken a liking to Rapunzel and often tried to show her new ways of creating biochemistry. The Hag cut corners and changed elements with the most exciting results. That is why Rapunzel tolerated her coming into her tower of isolation.

There was a united joy when one of these Hag potions produced a discovery in healing. Of course, the Hag was delighted to market a new product and rubbed her hands gleefully at the dollar signs going up in her bedraggled mind.

Rapunzel caught the Underground home. She was too tired to cook, so she stopped at the restaurant downstairs. The maître d', Dimitri, was keen on her and always sat her in the back corner, away from others. He saw she'd had a hard day and ordered her usual special vegan dish from the kitchen; she smiled at his understanding as he poured her a glass of water.

Across the room and two tables down was a man dressed in a soft grey three-piece tailored suit, with wavy blonde hair that fell over his right eyebrow. He called Dimitri over and asked who the long-haired beauty was in the corner.

The maître d' cleared his throat, saying reluctantly, "She is a biochemist, sir."

"Well, send her over a bottle of your finest champagne."

Dimitri made a noise in his throat like a humph and signalled to the waiter with the order.

Minutes later, the waiter arrived at Rapunzel's table with the champagne, explaining that it had been sent from the gentleman two tables up. Rapunzel blushed and felt suddenly angry, thoughts creating chaos as she struggled with the imposition.

"Please thank the gentleman." She rose from her booth. Picking up the bottle, she nodded to the man and headed to the young couple next to her. She handed them the champagne and said, "On the house."

They were delighted. Rapunzel returned to her seat but sat with her back to the gentleman, so she couldn't see him, tucking herself further into the booth, awaiting her meal.

Dimitri brought her dinner himself and rolled his eyes; she knew what he meant. She appreciated his kindness; he understood her need for solitude. Rapunzel lingered over her meal, enjoying the subtle flavours. When she rose to leave, the man was still there. She nodded as she passed him and kept walking, waving goodnight to the cook and smiling at Dimitri.

She climbed the stairs to her apartment and kicked off her shoes. Rapunzel walked out onto the balcony and brushed her long, golden hair. She preferred to plait it the entire length for sleeping. During the day, she plaited it down to her waist and wound that bit around her head, the rest hanging loosely like a ponytail, down to her knees. She loved the city lights as she spent time unwinding from her busy day and the intrusion of the Hag.

Rapunzel caught the Underground extra early the following morning, wanting to grab a coffee and read the paper before starting her new project. The Hag was getting agitated about the talk of a takeover bid for control of the company. Rapunzel arrived at work and was shocked to find the Hag in her laboratory with the blonde-headed man from last night. The Hag introduced him as Prince Pierre Grimm, the Thirty-second, the heir to the principality. Rapunzel stared at the man, aghast. The Prince demanded the Hag leave them; she winced, glared, and stormed out of the room.

"Rapunzel," said the Prince in sultry tones. "I am very impressed with your work here, and I have decided to keep you on as chief biochemist in the takeover process. On the other hand, the Hag is another matter entirely. I have big plans for the company and its franchises, and I intend to expand into Arabic countries and down to Australia."

The Prince was very sophisticated and in command, exuding confidence. Just then, a knock came on the door. An older gentleman wearing a black suit walked in carrying a tray with peppermint tea and savoury biscuits. Rapunzel could see he had researched what she liked to drink and eat.

"Apologies for last night; it never occurred to me that you don't drink alcohol," said the Prince with respect.

Rapunzel had gone all shades of pink and red and white. And the Prince was studying her as he handed her the tea. Her hand shook, and she put the tea down. Rapunzel was a person who considered her words carefully before saying anything. She sorted through a cacophony of feelings that marched through her head and left her reeling. The suddenness of this enormous change was beyond words. Rapunzel paced the room, vulnerable, not looking at him.

She spoke softly, "I lost my parents when I was born, I have a great fear of loss, and in essence, you just wiped out my reclusive world by entering that door with your elaborate, overwhelming plans".

The Prince looked apologetic and sat down on her desk seat. "I want you to come with me to all the franchises, acting as adviser to the biochemists in each country. Then we will put together a conference so that each franchise moves onto the same page. Will you think about it?"

Rapunzel looked at him, the turmoil of change plastered on her face. "And what of the Hag?"

"We have already spoken. The Hag will assume your role in this tower and be pretty happy, being left on her own as you have been; she doesn't like people."

Rapunzel felt the enormity of this. Was this what it takes to progress, to shift her view? Something in her came alive. Something that had been missing, thoughts of adventure and happiness filled her heart, and she laughed. This Prince, complete with butler, had swept into her space, sat in her chair and offered her the world. How could she say no?

"I'll think about it," she said dismissively.

Distant Fires

Marc Cannella

This story was awarded *First Prize*
in the short story category of the
Alice Sinclair Memorial Writing Competition.

I. PROLOGUE – The Divine Mistress of Guildford Manor (or, "A Re-Emergence")

Our heroine does not show herself. Discarded by her own capricious author, Celeste Wilford long ago became lost in the ether of fantasy, seemingly unfit for the trials and upheavals of fictional endeavour. The flighty, uncaring disposition of her creator eventually laid waste to her existence, for Celeste was not deemed worthy of novelistic capacities. Who knows how vast is the cemetery of unlived lives? Ruthlessness, it must be said, is a necessity of creation, but Celeste's strength has been underestimated, and she finds herself transcending her own limitations in a quest of observation and enlightenment that she has never been able to experience of her own accord. Now destined to roam the corridors of history, albeit contained within the walls of Guildford Manor, Celeste's privilege will become ours, too. This orphan of fiction is not yet done with the world.

It is not up to this author to disclose the exact nature of our dear Celeste's existential proportions, as enough has already been said of her spiritual peculiarities. It is her general guidance that is of much more interest to us in the telling of these following episodes. With her metaphysical traits obliquely explained to its satisfactory end, a more dispassionate account of her physical and intellectual attributes may be of necessity for some, and so a short description is presently in order.

Blessed with a pleasing countenance and lithe figure, Celeste Wilford nonetheless has not been able to rid herself of her slightly dishevelled tone of dress. Her white frock drags casually along the ground as she drifts from one place to the next, collecting black discolouration at the bottom and leaving a sense of untidiness to her otherwise clean attire. One may argue that it is unbecoming of a young lady to be in such a state, but in her case, not much can be done to reverse what has already been perpetually decided for her. Her agile and inquiring mind, though, is a great virtue and certainly suits the purposes of our objective. With the expository details fulfilled, we can now follow her to where she herself cannot be seen.

Contrary to what you, dear reader, may think, Celeste's circumstances are so far beyond out of her control as to be in the lap of the gods. She has never known choice, and she never will. The fog of her existence may be a blessing for us, as the conjuring of her state enables us to view long-gone occurrences at this grand English estate, Guildford Manor. But, due to the random nature of fate, these episodes are not always of a preferred variety, especially to Celeste, who is supposedly known to delight in the lighter aspects of life. And so it is with our first visit, to the 18th century, and the inner conflicts of Henry Colchester. Celeste peers with apprehension through a gap in the slightly open, heavy oak doors of the chapel, and this is what she perceived. The inhabitants of this particular moment in time, and some others to follow, will no longer be a mystery.

II. RELIGION, 1764 – In The Clergy (or, "Doubt")

The ecclesiastical tendencies of Henry Colchester asserted itself early in his life. The weekly church services attended by his whole family meant not only participating in the illumination of the word of God, but they also allowed him to bask in the sacred choral music which in no small part secured the good reputation of the township. It simply stirred his soul, and there was no doubt that he would devote his coming years to the clergy. On this day, however, Henry been called on to visit a certain Guildford Manor, in particular its appending chapel. This cloistered sanctuary served as both a communal outlet for those upholding Christian ritual, and also provided retreat and comfort for those whose faith garnered strength in solitude.

His previous association with the household meant his request was duly accepted from the current owner, Mr John Downe. The housekeeper led Henry across the front of the property towards the chapel, and he let himself in. With the formidable doors now behind him, and with the glaring sunlight now suitably shut out, he slowly and deliberately strode to the front-left corner of the second row of pews and knelt down. He bowed his head, and with his elbows spread apart on the top of the front seat, he clasped his hands together tightly.

The grey atmosphere and insufficient lighting could not hide the obviousness of Henry's anguish. He seemed so deep within himself as to be unaware of reality. As a practising clergyman, challenges of both practical and abstract natures were examinations that Henry had to regularly contend with. What he could not foresee was the insidious creeping in of doubt. His faith, his own personal cultivation of the mysterious, had recently woven into his mind knots of unwanted clutter, a tangle of thoughts determined to drive him to suspicion. Having known nothing of suffering himself, he started feeling unworthy of God's concern.

Thinking back briefly to former times, the remembrance of a particular incident refused to part with his conscience. Mr Downe's niece, Ms

Wordsworth, was a young woman of fine qualities, with a fairness of temperament coupled with the freshness of youth. She was a product, it must be said, of altogether good breeding, whose future was, if not yet secure, then on its way to achieving happiness and prosperity. A Mr Townsend of a nearby village, Bancroft, had all but won her heart, their courtship being one of sensitive interaction and veiled attraction. The declaration of mutual affection was imminent. That is until the dreadful illness that consigned Ms Wordsworth to an early, tragic demise, a fact still mourned by the whole of the town of Tealey. Evil is as natural as the good that tries to overcome it, but this was no evil act, it was pure bad luck. Good luck smells of roses and its scent can be ascertained from afar. But bad luck is a plague that imposes itself on unsuspecting victims.

The counsel offered by Henry Colchester to all those who loved her brought sobering consolation to them, but the young man struggled with a gnawing sense of inadequate justification for the miserable turn of events. The burden of shame and guilt was imposed upon him, with problematic questions to ponder. To be a merchant of faith without the necessary convictions is a sad state indeed, and leaves one bereft of resources to offer what is required by the community. After almost an hour in the pew of the chapel, Henry had willed himself to assert the strength of his conviction. After all, he thought with a tinge of optimism, if I were to summon Him at will for my own singular purpose, the divine mystery would be lost, and all affirmation of faith would cease. To endure is the non-negotiable obligation of this life.

One cannot help but sympathise with our Celeste, who had to bear the sight of poor Henry firsthand in that dark chapel, pondering the validity of his own existence and the apparent uselessness of his faith. When the scene was over and she retreated back into the obscurity of the shadows, Celeste was thankful that no such thoughts had ever intruded upon her own wellbeing. She figured that, perhaps, one cannot be well-adjusted unless one is inclined to at least some self-loathing. The heavy cloak of oppression was beginning to weaken her resolve, and so she left Henry Colchester to contemplate the deliciousness of his spiritual duty.

III. CLASS, 1818 – A Splash Of Decorum (or, "The Tea Incident")

Little known to the inhabitants of the residence, the daily serving of tea amounted somewhat to a highlight for the servants. The Stanthorpes regarded its staging as a tradition of utmost importance, a convention of such simplistic ritual as to appear unworthy of detailed observation to the uninitiated. If tradition is a form of social structure, then tea and scones must be allowed to be the height of dignified indulgence. Lady Charlotte Stanthorpe thought as much. "I love a biscuit. If a day goes by without one, I shall wither and die!" The Lady's untethered comments were tolerated by her husband, William, whose own appetite was more inclined towards supper and the winding down of the day's labours.

"You can't make a living without earning your supper," is what Lord Stanthorpe would say to his wife, who would happily, and frequently, spend her day without exerting herself unreasonably. And her response to her husband would be that of, "Nobody could begrudge the charms of a sedentary life," or something of the sort. And so a gentle tête-à-tête would ensue, for their banter was not simply a mere means of communication, but also a mental game of wits, with barbs of wordplay splintering the cosiness of their situation. If one has no-one to argue with, arguing with oneself is the only option after that, and a surer sign of madness has not yet been seen in this world.

In the afternoon, the Stanthorpes were enjoying their silence in the sitting room, while quietly anticipating how to navigate the dangers of potential topics of discussion. Meanwhile, Mrs Crutchley and the other maids were preparing the tea to be brought out to them. Thornley and

Walsh, impatient in their movement and unnecessarily quick in their step, entered the room ready to serve. With the trays in their hands and their heads full of eagerness to please, an unseen fold in the rug unexpectedly presented itself to their shuffling feet. What happened next you have probably guessed already, and with the tumbling of both ladies so did the tea and scones!

It all occurred as if in slow motion, with nothing left to do but wait for the effects of the spectacle to unfold. Cups turned into shards of confetti, and hot tea showered the floor, avoiding the extra embarrassment of collecting the Stanthorpes. Celeste, privy to the discourse but veiled from the attention of the party, cupped her hands in gleeful delight at this episode. With the maids feverishly cleaning up the mess, our sharp, bright light poking through the keyhole of history perched herself on the threshold. Of course, she could not be seen, but all in the room glanced at once into the same empty space, as if expecting someone to appear at any second at the door. But alas, nobody was there.

IV. NOBILITY, 1911 – A Gathering (or, "The Manuscript")

"Is it a comedy or a tragedy?" asked Lord Vernon. Holed up in the drawing room with his son-in-law, James, and the local barrister, Mr Burgess, the post-supper proceedings allowed for a freer dialogue and probing discussions that were not always appropriate for other times and other rooms. These men were now, at this moment, in their element and ready for the discourse to flow freely.

"It's both," said James, leaning with his elbow on the mantelpiece and wafting cigar smoke from his mouth in a casual fashion. "Its most unfortunate aspect is its sentimentality. Unforced pathos rings far truer, and I dare say this should be the aim of all artists, especially those whose craft depends on the written word."

"Ah. Having not yet acquainted myself with the work I shall take your judgement as fact for the time being," said the bold young man's father-in-law. The subject the three men were deliberating was that of a novella recently published by Lord Vernon's nephew, Tristan.

"It is an inescapable irony that the two should be so inextricably linked," said Burgess, with his plump frame couched comfortably in the sofa, legs crossed. His portly figure seemed to be made of beef and gravy, with his heft being both his hindrance and his distinction. "Indeed, I would argue, the greatest literary works have sought to explore their compelling correlation." A smile perched on the side of his mouth. It was undeniably a favourite topic of his, that of the cruel paradoxes of life itself. Burgess, the self-styled arbiter of democracy, may not have led a remarkable existence, but he did serve the perception of a well-functioning society very well through his occupation. That he was a man of great moral understanding was of no doubt; his taste in literature, however, was another matter.

Apparently, Vernon's nephew had discovered a half-finished manuscript in a chest surreptitiously located in a bedroom upstairs, which he had found while staying for the weekend at his distinguished uncle's house. Having read the unfinished work, Tristan was sufficiently taken by it to have a spirited go at completing it. With nothing to recommend him beyond his own keen feelings, he proceeded to fake some talent to bring closure to the beguiling story. Something about a young woman, name of Wordsworth.

"How morbid!" bellowed Burgess. "What wicked creations fester in the minds of so-called writers! What's more, the audacity to render such serious subject matter with wit. That should be left to those who have proved themselves to be worthy exponents of it." Lord Vernon and James stood silently in their positions, debating within themselves as to how forceful a response should be made to the man.

"I'm afraid the position you have taken is untenable, Burgess," Lord Vernon eventually said diplomatically. The room suddenly became stuffy and shrouded with mild tension. "There are two types of opinion, a right one and a wrong one, and I'm not going to say which category you find yourself in. I think you are in a muddle on this point."

James interjected. "Two types of opinion! I don't know if you mean that truthfully, sir, but all arguments call for nuance, which is where the quality of debate rests. As for Tristan's work, we should try to be constructive in our assessments. However, I can say it does not rank highly in my view. But thankfully his literary ambitions are not likely to scupper his more pressing plans."

"Well then," Burgess resignedly said with a barely audible huff, "I may have to concede my obstinacy as proof of my unmodern thoughts, and give young James my due. I am past the age of optimism. I'll leave that to the young so I can continue down the road of pessimism. You never know, some truth may lie there too."

V. EPILOGUE – Celeste Departs (or, "Ashes Into Dust")

Upheavals would soon spread like wildfire throughout Europe, but they will be distant fires to our dear Celeste. Despite her latest author's attempt to rescue her from the ashes of eternity, dust she must become.

The first stage of death is the loss of memory. Baffled by the burden of your own consciousness, you nonetheless existed in spite of time. But, eventually, time will be the death of you. Extinguished.

Night Feathers (Forgive Me)

Amy Purton-Long

The wild in you is at my back fence
and all my desperate windows
shine the moon at you in bursts of code.

If you could rescue me,
would you?
Dismantle me?
Into fragments of glass, crush my concrete bones
return me to your
timeless sands.

Would you disappear me?

I ask so much. Still,
my wandering mouth –
I have eaten the land and yet still
you are at the edges of me
your night feathers
lifted by wind,

silently crying for what we,
together
have lost.

Dawn stretches and the noise awakens
my SOS is swallowed by sun.
The wild in you
fades into
my roaring, thoughtless morning.

SECTION 2

LIVING WITH THE PAST ...

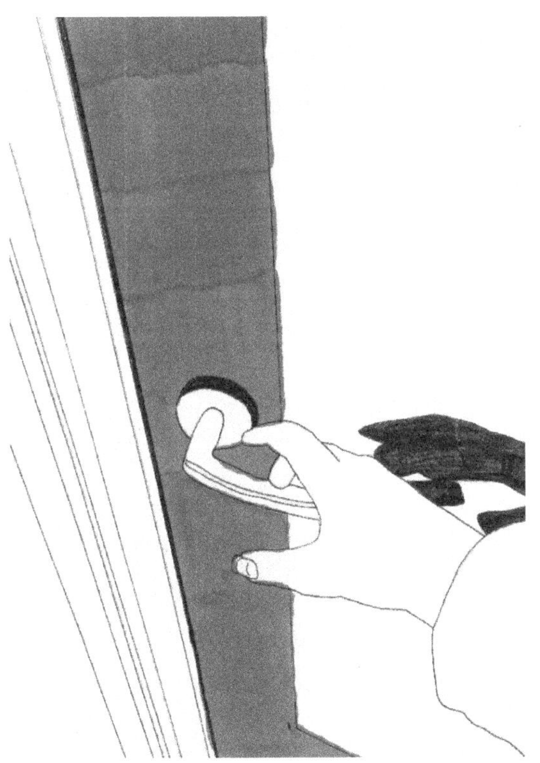

Boy With a Trumpet

Janice Williams

This poem was awarded *First Prize*
in the poetry category of the
Alice Sinclair Memorial Writing Competition.

(Lockdown, Anzac Day 2020)

A silver sunlight-thread
embroiders shadowed autumn night
as a boy lifts his trumpet
        Come home, come home

Last Post's silver notes
glint in predawn chill
awake an Anzac dawn
like no other

Candle-cupped hands
of brothers and sister
light his shadow
with glimmered hope
bright-sutured hope

Threads of old-new Anzac story
seam four children to Anzac tale
to past and future
to troops beneath white crosses
where row on row
bright poppies grow in far shell-stricken soil
of Flanders fields *
        Come home, come home

Blow stories bleak on Belgian winds
waft their tales
of brothers who came not home
of sisters who wept history-tears
till shadows lift in sunshine
and speak anew through children's tunes
and shine anew in children's eyes
        Come home, come home

Dawn lights the Anzac sky

* These lines refer to *In Flanders Fields* by John McCrae, May 1915

Not Like Him

Kylie Moppert

Marg arranged a selection of snacks from the antipasto platter her sister had prepared onto a dinner plate. Colourful marinated and raw vegetables with dried biscuits and hummus.

"Take some cheese and prosciutto," Liz said.

"Ha ha," Marg said without humour. "Don't suppose you have vegan cheese?" She waited for Liz's eye roll before taking the plate to the den, where Nathan, earphones on, huddled under a single lamp in the shadowed room. Long dark hair covered one side of his face giving him a waning moon look. He closed his journal and looked at her warily. Seeing the food, his face brightened. He dipped a broccoli floret in hummus and nodded thanks. Marg reached to touch him but he pulled away.

"Did he say thanks?" Liz said as Marg settled on the couch.

"As well as any thirteen-year-old."

"He should have gone with Pete and the kids. Bit of male time," Liz said.

"Vegans aren't into killing fish," Marg said, not looking at Liz.

"He didn't have to fish. Time with Pete would do him good."

"Ah yes, he'd like me telling him that, wouldn't he?"

"You need to show him who's boss."

"Leave it Liz. When yours are teenagers you'll get it."

"As long as they're under my roof I'll set the rules."

"Good luck with that. Are we watching this?" Marg indicated the TV, her face creased in irritation.

"I mean it, Marg. You let him get away with too much. Not having a dad shouldn't mean weak boundaries."

"He's got a dad." Marg sighed. "An absent one. We've seen this. Every episode." Marg reached for the remote but Liz grabbed it, holding it out of Marg's reach.

"You chose last week," she said. "Anyway, I never remember the ending." Liz laughed with genuine amusement.

Marg rolled her eyes. "I'm not giving into your sulking." Liz picked up their glasses, passing Marg hers. "Drink," she said. "Relax. Enjoy."

They watched in silence. Half an hour in, Liz suggested it was the priest.

"Keep guessing," Marg said.

"Don't tell me," Liz picked up the bottle and went to refill Marg's glass.

"Not for me. Gotta drive."

"Go on, you need it."

Marg held her hand over her glass. "Need my licence more."

Liz filled her own glass to within a finger of the rim.

"Speaking of priests, are you following the Royal Commission?"

"Hard to miss."

"Coz I was thinking, didn't Syl board at St Joseph's?"

Marg looked at her sister, her eyes flicked toward the den and back.

"Has he answered Nathan's letter?" Liz asked.

Marg shook her head. "I don't know if he's still at that address. Nathan sent one care-of Agnes last week. She called – hasn't seen him in years."

"A mother's worst nightmare." Liz shuddered.

"Yeah well, it's no picnic for Nathan."

"No." The women fell silent. "He'll turn up. He always does," Liz said.

"In times of crisis. Syl's crisis. Always his."

"So – no news is good news."

"Try telling Nathan that," Marg said. "For three years."

At 10:15 the next morning, Marg wanted a cigarette. She hadn't smoked for months – perhaps a year. She didn't think of herself as a smoker, but she enjoyed the smell, and the desire never really left her.

In times of stress she was inclined to relapse.

"Why can't I know?" Nathan, leaning against the sink, glowered at her from under his hair. Still in pyjamas, eyeliner and sleep accentuated his pale complexion.

"I don't know myself," Marg said. She sipped tea, tapping a pen on her shopping list. "Do you want cereal, peanut butter?"

"Gran would know."

"Please don't ask her, Nate." She wrote *biscuits* on her list. "She's old, and already distressed with Syl missing for so long."

"I have a right to know."

"Nate, leave it." Marg took her cup to the sink.

Nathan slid sideways, away from her as she approached. Secondary school, now hormones – Marg worried she was losing him. She rinsed her cup. "Syl boarded somewhere when Agnes was unwell. For a term, maybe. Will you help me with shopping?" She slung her handbag over her shoulder, picked up her list and examined it. "Any special requests? For lunch?" When Nathan didn't answer she turned. "Nathan, don't call Agnes. Your rights don't include opening old wounds."

Marg returned her empty trolley and went back into the supermarket. She walked down the cereal aisle, eyeing the sugar-coated options. When Nathan was little and Syl visited, he'd bring a box, wrapped in plain paper, once in newspaper. Marg would never buy sugary cereal, but she couldn't stop Syl bringing it on his rare visits. Syl had been missing for a year when Marg wrapped a box in Santa paper and put it under the tree. As Nathan unwrapped it and saw what it was he dropped the package and ran through the house, calling out for his father. Marg shuddered, remembering her shame. She walked through to the freezer where she chose vegan fish fingers. At the checkout she bought menthol cigarettes featuring before and after photos of a cancer victim. The man looked dead in the after photo. She shoved them in her handbag with Nathan's treat.

"Give me a hand, Nate?" Marg called as she lugged shopping inside. She put everything away and the kettle on then walked from room to room, looking for him. She messaged him — *Vegan Fish Fingers for lunch xx*. At noon she rang him, but it went straight to voicemail. She smoked outside where a patch of sunshine promised more than it delivered. *Football.* Nathan no longer played, but his mate Hamish did.

Marg saw Hamish on the field, black mud from hip to shoulder. She raised her collar against the wind and scanned faces, but couldn't see Nathan. She was about to ask someone when she spotted Nathan sitting in the stand. He was with a bunch of kids, talking to someone behind him, his body twisted toward them, away from her. Wearing his Nirvana t-shirt, apparently unaffected by the late winter chill. She yearned to give him her jacket, instead she returned to her car, clutching her keys in her pocket.

Marg checked her phone as the winter light faded and clouds thickened. At 4:46 she called Hamish's home. "Hello Julie, Marg here. I'm sorry to bother you. Is Nathan with Hamish?" Marg listened, heard her call out to Hamish, ask him about Nathan.

"Marg, Hamish hasn't seen him all day."

"But he was at the game. I saw him." Again, Marg heard Julie speaking to the room behind her.

"No, Marg. Hamish didn't see him. Perhaps he's with his cousins?"

"Of course. He'll be there. Thanks, Julie." She hung up, fist clenched, nails digging into her palm.

Syl had insisted he didn't want children, but Marg, in her eagerness, dismissed his reasons: *The world's overcrowded. I've got wonky genes.* One she couldn't believe: *I'd be a crap dad.* This with his crooked grin, tugging her ear and kissing her jawbone. *You've got an edge,* he'd say.

When she suspected pregnancy, Marg kept quiet. She wore underwear and a liner to bed when her period was due. As her breasts grew she loosened her bra-straps, but the cups squeezed her, creating bulges and a cleavage she didn't recognize. Bold blue veins appeared, aggressively lacing her breasts. She wore big jumpers, hid her chest behind her arms.

The week after her second missed period Syl spooned behind her in bed, one breast cupped in his hand.

"Your breasts are like light bulbs."

"Must be getting my period," she said, wriggling her bum into his groin.

Syl sat up, turned on the light and asked her straight.

Marg rolled over to look at him. She bit her lip, watching his Adam's apple ripple. "I don't know. Maybe."

His eyes narrowed, lip curled. "You stopped taking the pill." He thrust his chin forward, as though shoving her.

Marg shrank from him. Then Syl was out of bed, tugging on clothes and gone.

Marg was pacing her back porch, smoking her second cigarette when her phone vibrated and the tango started.

"I'm bored," Liz said. "Will you two come for pizza?"

"Nathan's missing."

Liz fired questions Marg couldn't answer.

"It's not like him to disappear," Marg said.

"Unlike his dad."

"Maybe he's gone to Syl's place," Marg said.

"I thought he didn't live there anymore."

"I don't know that. The letter wasn't returned." Marg stubbed her cigarette out. "I'll go and see." As she drove to St Kilda her phone glowed in her bag, the tango drilling into the back of her skull. Liz and Marg shared the ring tone, a nod to dance classes years prior. She shoved her bag at the floor where the contents spilled. The phone vibrated free, twisting about like a dying blowfly. She flicked the radio on, switching from music to voices, needing someone else's conversation. A man's deep voice, deliberate cadence, coaxed Marg into his story. *'What many don't realise, is how pervasive this behaviour was, and how many people's lives were tragically affected.'* It was several minutes before Marg realised what he was talking about.

In St Kilda Marg drove loops looking for a park. She was waiting to turn right when she saw Nathan, walking away from her, down Fitzroy Street. Marg stopped mid-intersection, indicated her need to change direction. Car horns blared, refusing her. Her phone glowed, the tango twanged. Marg swore, finished her turn and did an illegal U-turn, bumping over the tram separation kerb. By the time she was heading south, watching the pavement more than the road, her head was pounding. But it was someone else's son, too young to be slouching alone as daylight faded.

Marg parked a block away. She checked her reflection. Her face was flushed. She applied lipstick, stirred her hair, patting her face as though with a cool washer. She didn't want to see

Syl. Of all people, not the Latin woodman. Admitting Nathan was missing to Syl would make her nightmare real.

Marg looked at Syl's window. Light glowed through a blanket, sagging in the middle. It blocked any view within, such as it would be. She crossed with the walk lights and approached the front door, held open with an electric iron. A stub of wires, like a frayed rope, sprouted where the lead had been cut. There was no-one around. Empty beer bottles littered the stairwell. Marg picked her way upstairs. She knocked. The door cracked open and Marg saw a grey faced woman with long pale hair.

"I'm looking for Sylvester."

The woman shook her head, eyes large.

"Is he here? Do you know where he is? I'm looking for my — our son …" The door was closing. Marg thrust her foot forward, keeping it wedged. She craned her neck, peering into the shadows. "Please, have you seen him? Do you know where Syl is?"

"Git out, git out, *git*." The woman's voice croaked. Marg heaved into the door and released her foot. She limped downstairs, cursing.

In her car she checked her phone. Liz's messages, each more urgent than the last. The battery indicator glowed red. Marg lit her third cigarette and touched the green phone. She spoke as soon as Liz answered. "He's not here. No Syl either." Marg sucked her cigarette.

"Call the police."

"I will. From home. Don't call. I can't answer while I'm driving and I'm sick of the bloody tango."

It was after six when Marg got home and readied herself to call the police. As she plugged her mobile in to charge Liz rang. "Have you called them?"

"I'm about to. Hang on, that's the landline."

"Don't hang up —"

"Hello?"

"Hello Marg."

"Agnes?"

"He's here."

Marg closed her eyes, she sighed, holding the receiver to her chest, taking a moment to release her tension, absorb her relief. She brought the receiver back to her ear.

"... you need to come, he wants to see you."

"Yes, yes, of course. Oh Agnes. I'll come now."

"Tomorrow is fine."

"No no. I'll come now."

"It's a long way, Marg."

"I'm leaving now."

Marg hung up, calling Liz with an update as she climbed into the car.

Two hours up the freeway, Marg stopped for fuel and a greasy meal. She recalled, again, her conversation with Agnes. She wanted to call, speak with Nathan, but her phone had died. In any event Agnes' number wasn't in her phone. She bought mints, resisting a fourth cigarette. An hour later on the narrow country road she drove carefully, wary of kangaroos and stray livestock.

At 10:20pm the main street of Agnes' country town was quiet; a straggle of locals smoking outside the pub, youths bouncing skateboards around the civic park.

Heading out of town to Agnes' place Marg saw a kid, shoulders hunched, wearing a hoody, walking alone amongst shadows. She slowed, peering at the figure as she passed. He turned into a laneway, skipping over a puddle. She drove up the hill to Agnes' home.

The cottage was dark except for the porch light. Marg cupped her hand in front of her mouth, smelling mint.

"Hello Agnes," she said, unsure if she should kiss her. During Marg and Syl's brief marriage, the women had met less than a dozen times. Agnes sent Nathan birthday and Christmas cards with money, but the women seldom spoke and hadn't seen each other in years. Despite her slight frame, her white hair, withered skin, Marg was intimidated by her ex-mother-in-law.

"Come in. He's asleep." Agnes pointed to a closed door, indicating Marg should be quiet.

Marg stepped into the dark hall, following Agnes to the kitchen. Agnes waved Marg to a seat and filled the kettle.

"I can't believe he came here." Marg said, looking back down the hall to the closed door.

"It's his childhood home," Agnes said. As she spoke Marg watched the door open and a figure emerge from the shadows.

"Syl. Oh Jesus." Marg turned to Agnes. "I ... Nathan. I thought you meant Nathan." She slumped into a seat, her head in her hand.

"Nathan?" Syl said from the kitchen doorway.

"Since this morning." Marg was biting her fist, fear constricted her throat. "Three times I thought —" she stopped, looked at Syl. "I did though. I saw him in the village. I think. It might not be him, but it might." She was down the hall and out the door before Agnes or Syl could say anything. Her hands trembled as she started the ignition. Then Syl was climbing in the passenger side, coat and boots in hand.

"I'll come," he said. His skin was grey, his face gaunt, a frail version of his former self. "You stay, Mum. If he turns up someone needs to be here."

As Marg drove toward the village she was relieved to have Syl beside her. Available, finally, for a crisis other than his own. But she wished it was Syl's crisis. Not Nathan's. Not hers. Not *theirs.*

Ghosts

Roslyn Varley

This story was awarded a *Highly Commended* in the short story category of the Alice Sinclair Memorial Writing Competition.

Night:

Alone in the old farmhouse. Alone in the kitchen … Anne sips her whisky. She shuffles her cards, for another game of Solitaire.

Some of the cards spill to the Laminex, and some slide further along the yellow-swirled pattern, and tip to the floor. She leans to scoop them from the worn lino — all brown and green squares, cracked and gritty underfoot.

Anne rights herself, puffing on cards to remove any grit … and pauses mid-puff: there's a wispy figure across the table … a woman … with a tangle of grey hair.

Her *mother*?

Anne shuts her eyes and shakes her head. She shuffles for more time.

"You'll shuffle the tits off the Queen."

It certainly sounds like her mother.

Anne opens one eye to check her whisky bottle … she'd only had two nips for goodness' sake … hallucinating now?

But her mother's still sitting there!

Anne opens both eyes and focuses on the cards in her shaking hands. Nevertheless, she feels the moment requires some comment. She says quietly to her cards, "I'm always thorough with shuffling." Then she looks across the Laminex.

Her mother's holding a flaming match to a cigarette.

Anne thinks, *Get a grip on yourself.* But with heart skittering she sends seven cards across the swirling pattern to … to her mother? And seven for herself, though her grip with sweaty fingers makes it difficult to sort them into some sort of order.

Her mother calmly sorts her cards, then frowns. She says, "You might as well get a cart and go dealing."

Oh yes, her mother used to say that one too. Anne smiles at the old expression, heard so often during all those visits back to the farm. *In the past.*

"Mum, it's … it's so good to … see … you?"

Her mother leans in over the Laminex. "It's good to see you too Anne. You're looking well, if a little pale." She sits back into the aura of smoke drifting from her cigarette.

Mum's sipping whisky now.

"Enjoying my single malt, Mum? Better than the cheap stuff we used to drink. How you lived to ninety-three I don't know."

"Smoked and pickled," Mum says. "Should've lasted forever."

Anne puts down three tens.

Mum snorts, "Already?"

"And three Sevens."

Her mother peers at her cards, and frowns, and mutters, "Oh what to do to be saved."

Anne smiles, and says, "It seems you *were* saved."

She leans an elbow on the table, chin in hand. She thinks, yes there she is, in some way, her mother, in her old grey-blue dressing-gown. The cigarette was now balancing precariously in an ashtray.

"Mum, you've got an afterlife of sorts? You must have believed in something. Something ...?"

Her mother sniffs, looking up from her cards. "Believed in nature. Sunsets. Believed in poems and plays and books. And jokes of course. Believed in quiet thoughts ... unlike your father." She downs her whisky. "I suppose he's gone too?"

"He died a few years after you. At ninety-seven. But you'll know that, being a ghost?"

"No ... I didn't know." Mum picks up the bottle and asks Anne if she wants another.

"No thanks Mum ..."

"Why not? There a drought on?"

Anne smiles at her mother's old line.

Her mother pours herself a generous shot. "My funeral ... at the graveside?"

"Yes."

"Good."

Anne takes a deep breath, and traces with a finger the yellow swirls and curls on the Laminex. "Dad's casket ... it went in on top of yours."

Mum gulped her shot of whisky. She carefully put down her glass. "An oversight by you and your brother perhaps?"

"Oh Mum we should've talked about that with Noel before you died, shouldn't we? I'm sorry." Anne begins to reach a hand across to her mother, but strokes the tabletop instead. "It's a good spot out there in the scrub, under the great white gums. And now your old mate Ted's there in the next row."

"Good old Ted. We had some lively talks over the years."

"His headstone's behind yours. Could almost have a chat."

"And your father'd drone on about his overseas travels." Mum drops three aces to the table: spades, clubs, diamonds.

"You could've gone on those overseas trips Mum," Anne says gently.

Her mother squashes her cigarette in the ashtray. She lights another from her pack of Kools, drawing hard and then bathing them both in menthol. "Who wants to fall down a sewage drain in some god-forsaken country. And my gardens would've died."

"Noel would've looked after the gardens."

"The gardens." Mum leans back and watches the upward drift of smoke, its slow curl. "I used to sit by my veggie patch and watch those beautiful sunsets ... gold light flooding the valley ... the mountains cutting the horizon ... the sun sinking behind them. I used to think, why look for more beauty than here?"

Silence.

Until Anne says, "When your casket went down, the currawongs called from the trees."

Her mother taps the long ash from her cigarette ... just in time.

Anne says, "There was a huge turn-out for your funeral. And a write-up in the Clarion about your tennis, the Dramatic Society, Hospital committee, bridge. And your seventy-year marriage begun in the war years."

Mum places down three queens, one by one. "This a history lesson?"

Anne pours herself some water, sloshing it a little.

"Mum ... we're selling the farm. Settles in four weeks." She runs a finger round the rim of her glass, raising a small squeak. "Do you mind?"

Her mother leans forward into the faint screen of her cigarette smoke. "Should I mind — I'm apparently dead and gone." She pokes at her tangled hair with her remaining card — Anne sees it's the last ace.

Her mother eases out of her chair, and slowly moves to the cane couch at the end of the room. She looks to the window above it — with its dark night view to the north paddock.

Anne from her chair watches the small figure, and feels anew a longing for her mother … five years since she'd died.

"You and Dad were going to build in that north paddock, weren't you, after the War? You even made a garden there and walked each day in the heat of summer to water it. But after the War, Nanna and Pa moved away, leaving you to this old house."

Her mother still looks to the window. Then, she bends to pick up one of the couch cushions, faded and floral. She gives it a shake, and places it down again. She shrugs her shoulders. "Another history lesson?"

"After you died, Dad showed me where you began that garden, over there."

"Ah, he thought of me."

"Yes Mum, he thought of you."

Her mother drifts back and stands by her chair.

"Mum, maybe you knew we're selling *Sunnyvale* … that's why you've come? Perhaps a disturbance — up in the sky — over the farm?"

Silence.

Anne drops her final card to the tabletop. "What am I saying? I DON'T BELIEVE IN GHOSTS."

"Better believe it," says Mum, still standing. "You couldn't have drunk that much whisky on your own. And I'm not the only ghost hovering over this farm."

"Dad's ghost?"

"No, never him … probably hovering overseas, reliving his adventures up some river."

Anne laughs. "How often have we heard about that?" She leans in, "And what about Nanna and Pa?"

"Yes. Nelly was dancing, just like she used to … after Pa died." Her mother poured herself another nip.

"But I saw other ghosts Anne. Black ghosts … The men from when I first came here — they used to walk all the way from that old Mission. Come down our north paddock, over the creek, across the flatland, past this house. Worked at a farm up the Lane."

Anne says, "This beautiful place might have been their country … once … the hills and creeks and flatland … The high stony ground, the rubble of that ancient lava flow …"

"Ahh, an ode you're composing."

"Mum we know this land so well too. Our home for so long. Nanna and Pa coming in their wagon long before Dad was born. Now sold, after all these years."

Her mother moves back to the couch. She rearranges the floral cushion. Anne pictures her mother as she used to sit there on the couch, smoking, reading, with morning sun streaming in on her, cup of tea or coffee on the yellow stool beside her.

"Yes," her mother says, "Sold after all these years."

Silence.

"The furniture's going tomorrow, Mum."

Suddenly, her mother turns. "And your big wardrobe?"

"Yes, all the furniture."

Again, "And your big wardrobe?"

"Yes, Mum. Very heavy though."

"And your room, you'll check it … all over … when your wardrobe's gone?"

"Check my empty room?"

"Including under."

"Under what? The carpet?"

Her mother nods. She turns back then, to kneel on the couch. She leans to the window, peering out. "Stars are bright tonight. They're hanging low." With her final card, she taps the windowpane.

Anne comes to kneel beside her. Their arms brush, gently — the dressing-gown's satiny sheen strokes against the soft wool of Anne's jumper … a soft caress, almost not there. But it *is* there, and Anne feels a little jolt in her heart.

Her mother says again of the stars, "On nights like this when there's no moon, the stars are marvellous, spangling and silver sharp in the dark."

After a moment, she shuffles back, leaving the couch.

Anne stays with her nose against the cold glass, and blinks away tears. After a few moments she asks again about her bedroom.

"What am I checking for Mum, in my empty bedroom?"

"Mum?" There was no answer. She turns, "Mum?"

Mum isn't there.

Anne goes to check outside the door, on the small back verandah. *Of course,* Anne thinks, *she isn't going to be there. Isn't going to be anywhere. Of course not.*

She comes back into the kitchen.

There is no second glass, no cigarettes, no ashtray.

But her mother's final card is there, on the corner of the Laminex.

"Mum?"

Day:

Alone at the front gate ... Anne watches the removal van lumber off in a swirl of afternoon dust and heat. She looks bleakly at the gardens to her left and right, laced with weeds. The roses still bloomed bravely. She reaches for a yellow rose and strokes its petals, wishing she could conjure up her mother.

There'd been nothing under the carpet in her bedroom. Not under the wardrobe corner, or any corner. Of course not.

She drifts back inside. Then squaring her shoulders, she takes to the vacuuming with a vengeance. Around her old bedroom she goes with the machine, then Noel's old dark room, then around the musty loungeroom. Anne drives on into her parents' bedroom, with its screen door view over the wide front verandah, and the gardens.

At a corner of the carpet, where her mother's small wardrobe had been, the vacuum cleaner whined. She cut the motor. Something was poking out now, where the patterned navy carpet gave way to green lino at its edge. She drops to her knees.

She carefully withdraws an envelope. She feels the blood pounding in her ears. On the front is her mother's handwriting:

Anne your father told me to throw this out, but I couldn't. It's up to you what you do with it. You're the history buff.

She sits back, leaning against the wall. She re-reads her mother's words, breathing deeply to calm herself now. She looks out the screen door, watching two sparrows hop about on the verandah, listens to their chirps. And she hears the cawing of a crow somewhere over the flatland … until it grows fainter, and is lost.

Anne looks again at her mother's message. She slides two sheets of thin, fragile paper from the envelope: a letter, yellowed with age. It's dated 1917, and she senses herself holding history in her hands.

She reads the neat, cursive handwriting of her grandmother, Nelly.

Sunnyvale
4th December, 1917

Dear Sister,

There has been so much rain here. And the flooding, I never thought I would need to wish away rain! But it finally stopped, and our creek has gone down now.

Harry has been repairing the old house near the flatland. It will have to do for a home for a while as there is so much work with clearing and fencing.

Gracie my dear, I must tell you of Harry's discovery. Please tell no-one. As he checked our creek after the flood, Harry found bones in the newly exposed bank. Many human bones! At first, a skull, and as he dug, three more — and one was small. And all intermingled as if thrown in haste in a shallow pit. They must have once been further from the creek which has now cut a new course.

Harry is an anxious man. He does not want this taint of death on our soil to become common knowledge. He has reburied the bones, where our fences form a corner on a rise, well back from the creek.

He will erect a shed over the spot. He says it will be useful for storing the hay for our small flock.

Harry says of the bones that it is old history now. Our land now.

I'm not to tell anyone Gracie, but I must at least share my thoughts with you, my dear sister, so far from me.

Harry repeats that what happened here is before our time. Not our business. He is not a man to argue with as you know.

And he has prayed over them.

What is to be done?

I hope I have an opportunity to post this letter, but until then it will be safe in the lovely book you gave me on our departure.

For now, I'm your homesick and troubled sister, who sends you all her love.

Nelly.

Anne leans back and gently bumps her head against the bedroom wall, *thump, thump* on the cream fibro. Near the screen door the two sparrows still hop and chirp. She stares out over the verandah, and over the gardens, to the flatland shimmering in the heat. Then returns to the letter and reads again, and again.

And re-reads her mother's message.

Closing her eyes, Anne thinks about her mother. And her Nanna. She thinks about her father. And *his* father … and … And the *silences*.

Until her mobile jangles.

"Yes Noel everything … in the house … is gone. We'll talk when I get back to your place."

Placing the phone down on the carpet, she says softly, "A long, long talk."

She stares at the strip of green lino beside her at the base of the wall, and watches a silverfish slip along it and disappear beneath the worn-out carpet.

Anne decides to take a walk … over the flatland, across the creek, up into the north paddock, to the old shed.

84

The Parts that Hurt

Sarah Bennett

I am looking for the light.

But it's raining, and there is none. I open the window to let cold air clear out the stuffy house and the breeze cuts between my shoulders, the chill spinning through the exit wound in my back. I grab a cardigan from my suitcase and wrap it around my body, trapping my long hair. I am aching for warmth. I am aching to be whole again.

The funeral was meant to be my closure, not a bullet reminding me of all I am without.

I'm thankful for the rain, in the least. The drought has gone on two years too long. There are no more tears left in me to mourn the flower gardens that used to bloom that have now been plucked, plucked, plucked, until nothing but dead grass remains. Like my heart, plucked, plucked, plucked until the wound is bled dry, the earth has nothing left to give, not until the sky offers itself again.

I shake my hair loose from the cardigan, let it drape freely down my back. Gran used to have long hair, years before I was born. She looked so free. I look like her, how she was.

I am about to grab my brush to untangle the strands when an indistinct figure walks up the driveway, knocks on the door. He's elderly, and holding an umbrella, and his eyes are softening. He knew Gran.

"Hello?"

A dull ache blooms around the hole in my chest.

"Frank," the man says. "The gardener. I've been looking after the yard while Edith's been in the nursing home."

In my mind's eye I see him trimming the lavender, keeping it from growing wild into the grass. Keeping it growing tall and strong. When I was young, I didn't understand that cutting something back was for its own good. But the lavender thrived, always thrived under the gentle hand of Gran, and then the man standing in front of me.

"Of course, Frank. Thank you. I'm Olivia, her granddaughter."

The rain is a welcome change. A necessary change. By Frank's foot is the first stem of lavender, climbing to meet the drops. It's a miracle they kept themselves alive these past months.

"I'm sorry about it all. Real shame. She was lovely, she was. She was — lovely. Nice to me, always ready for a chat. Very lovely."

He talks as though he's found the meaning of life, talks as though the meaning of life is in giving to someone else, talks as though giving to someone else fills you up, too.

"She appreciated your work," I say. "She trusted you. Even when she wasn't around." It's been a dry season, the kind where grass crumples, thinner than paper, and flowers forget how to breathe. Frank hasn't had much to look after, but what was offered to his care was solemnly tended to. "She could never bring herself to sell this place, even with no one to live in it."

Despite going into a nursing home, she was adamant about not selling the house. Now it's a home to my grief, to me. My grief and I are one, I am nothing but empty.

This time next week I'll be driving back home, to my real home, where grief will lie dormant. I will cry, but in secret. In my car, maybe, or the shower. The tears will take me by surprise because my mind will not be thinking of her. I will have nothing to constantly taunt me and bring it up, like this house, this garden, this man.

I wonder if the wound in my chest will open again once I'm no longer here, where she was. As though the wound knows its cause.

"She kept it going for a long time, Edith. Respected hard work. Lovely woman."

My phone vibrates in my back pocket. Once, twice. My heart leaps, wanting to talk to Mum, the woman who can — or wants to — understand anything I go through, anything I feel. She held my hand throughout the funeral, squeezed it tight as a reminder that we are still alive, we are still here.

I slide it out from my pocket, just enough to see the notification.

It's Michael. Michael, who says he loves me. Michael, who didn't go to the funeral because the hour-long drive was 'too far'. Michael, who drives an hour every Sunday to walk on the beach.

Frank clears his throat. Frank, the man who came to see me in my grief. "Well, I just wanted to pay my respects. You won't be needing me here anymore, will you?"

There's a lump in my throat, so I offer my hand and clasp his own. It's over in a second; I let go of his clammy hands and swallow the lump, forcing it into my stomach where it turns to butterflies. This is where grief meets anxiety.

I quickly pull my long brown hair into a bun at the nape of my neck. Something to do, something to distract. I look like her, I look like her.

Once upon a time she would smooth my hair down, her aged fingers combing through the strands. This is how she loved me. She would tuck my hair behind my left ear, and I would keep it like that all day. This is how I loved her.

"You're very kind. Thank you." I fold my arms together. "Once the solicitors go through the will, we'll sell it. I just wanted a chance to go through her things by myself."

Frank twists his body slightly, a hint he's about to leave. Tea should have been offered. A biscuit tin opened. But I can't stand it, the small talk, all politeness and watery smiles. The mention of Gran — Edith — every few minutes as though we can keep her alive by saying her name. And even if I wanted to talk, Michael's text is the brain fog I can't see past, is the racing of my heart that stilts conversation.

"The lavender is going alright," Frank comments, an attempt to make us forget the reason for his visit.

It doesn't work, but the hole in my chest is a little smaller. Or perhaps it has simply become a shared space, a little less lonely. Maybe I need to plant some lavender there and fill my body with flowers, with sweetness, with something good. Something to make me whole again. Something to keep me going once Frank walks away.

"It was good of you to stop by."

He disappears into the grey, dull veil of rain. It's coming down fine, the drops small, a continuous sheet of water folding down over the house.

It was good of him to stop by.

I don't close the door; instead, I pull out my phone and open Michael's text.

Give me a call, whenever you're free. I've got something important to tell you, something very important. I love you, still.

Still, as though I'm damaged somehow. Still, as though he's doing me a favour by loving me.

My cardigan is thin, yet I don't feel the rain when I stand under it. It continues to water Gran's garden, the garden I will always consider to be hers. The lavender, hers. No matter who else lives here, who tends to the flowers, it will always belong to Gran.

It was ours though, together, in the holidays when I would visit, and the lavender was always happy. So was I.

I would hide amongst it, only I did not have to shrink myself down to fit there. I would simply sit while Gran was weeding and find my heart beating in time with the earth.

I bend down, pluck lavender from the dirt. I am looking for the light.

I miss being young enough to lie with the flowers. I miss not knowing that people die and don't come back. I miss being twelve, when being understood was more important than being kissed, when being heard was more important than being desired.

I miss being alone, with no one to disappoint me when they don't come to the funeral I've dreaded my whole life.

Some of my hair escapes the bun and sticks to my cheeks. Michael wouldn't like me like this.

I look at my phone again, reread the text he sent. Reread the *still.* Still, he loves me. But not enough to handle my grief. But not enough to comfort me. But not enough to say sorry about losing Gran.

But not enough.

There in the rain, I tap out a reply. Raindrops bounce off my phone screen, making it hard to type out the message I need to send. Maybe it would be hard anyway.

I do not expect him to respond.

There's a park near Gran's, the opposite direction of the beach. It overlooks the lake, one where men gut fish and pelicans hover, hoping for a catch. The lake is usually still, the water a serene mirror to the sky.

By the water are two swings, lonely, together. Gran would join me, then when she was too frail, Mum. Not Michael, never Michael. I think he's too dignified for that sort of thing. But I also don't think I would ever give him the chance to sit beside me and watch the water. I bled out the day she died, and I can't force Michael back into the gaping emptiness of my chest.

A few months ago and I would have tried. But a few months ago, I had forgotten the scent of lavender.

When I walk back inside, I search the linen cupboard. Worn towels, ripped sheets. Gran didn't throw much away but kept everything until it couldn't be used anymore. She believed in second chances, third chances, two thousand chances.

Mum and I visited Gran a few months ago, when she was still in the nursing home. We cleared out a lot of the rubbish, mostly cracked containers and rusted cutlery from the kitchen. We left the linen cupboard for another time, thinking we would be back on a holiday, filled with energy to spend sorting out the other rooms and visiting Gran when the summer heat made it too hot to shuffle furniture around.

I didn't expect to be here so soon. I didn't think that would be the last time —

But that's how it usually goes, isn't it? That's one part of history that repeats itself, isn't it?

My hands clasp around what I'm looking for, behind washers and handtowels. An old, empty vase standing at the back of the cupboard.

I wipe it down, set it on the kitchen table. I trim the stems of lavender, pull away the dead petals. The lavender suffered from the drought. The lavender is going alright. I might be crying. I might be okay.

The vase is bursting with purple, and the scent lingers. It says there's more to me than the parts that hurt.

The light, it is here.

Son of Prometheus

Ned Stephenson

This story was awarded *Second Prize* in the short story category of the Alice Sinclair Memorial Writing Competition.

My hands shook when filling the bag and now there's dust on my shoes and across the tiles. People are not as superstitious these days as in my mother's time. Yet for me, missing the bag is an omen I cannot ignore. There's quite a bit of dust in the pan, so rather than tip the sweepings in with the rest, I take it into the garden.

Already the lawn needs mowing again. My son can deal with it when he visits because rain is forecast, and now is not the time for me to be working in the heat. Peter will need to come more often if he's to stay on top of it.

Feeling the grass underfoot, I decide not to flick the pan onto the lawn. Instead, I make a circuit through the trees and past the rows of sun-wilted vegetables until I reach the orchard. There's a better spot under the lemon tree my husband planted for my gin 'n tonics. Perhaps the dust will return some life to the yellowing leaves.

Now that the gods are appeased, I return to the house, collect what remains in the bag, and set off to visit the potter.

The potter's shed sleeps in a gully of ancient tree ferns and towering mountain ash. People have talked about a potter in this valley for as long as I can remember.

Taking care not to slip on the gravel path down to where he works; I wonder to myself why I've never met him before. Well, today is the day to correct that and ask if he does commissions.

Beneath the potter's heavy eyelids, his eyes are kind and peaceful. "Sometimes I do special requests," he says. "What do you fancy?"

"I'm after bowls, like those you have over there. Only deeper, and a set of three."

He doesn't bother turning to see where I've pointed behind him.

"Large potage bowls? Sure, any colour in mind?"

"Dark blue. Like deep ocean water." I had imagined he would be older. It's hard to tell his age.

The potter scratches through his beard at the underneath of his chin. "I have cobalt bowls at the gallery in town. A little smaller and a set of four." He looks at me as though caught in a memory, then adds, "You'd have a spare."

I hold out my bag of dust before me.

"I'd like new ones, please. Will you put this in the glaze for me?"

The potter unties the bag and rubs the dust between his fingers. They remind me of my husband's hands, with pronounced veins and coarse hairs. There's no sign of a ring. I guess he wouldn't wear one while he worked with clay and water.

"What is it?"

"It's from my house."

His fingers keep judging the earth's properties. "It's gritty." He goes to dab some on his tongue. I flinch. He stops.

"I'll mill it smoother." He says as he frowns. "Though it may change the colour of your bowls."

His eyebrows have stripes of white in them, like a badger. He knows I'm looking at them.

"Please use it all. And only three bowls."

A long pause is filled by the distant rumble of approaching rain.

"When can you make them?"

This time he looks over his shoulder at the shelves covered with plates, vases, and bowls.

"Come back in a week."

That afternoon, the potter selects a block of pure white earthenware. He hums a psalm as he kneads the clay into a spiral many times over. When satisfied the clay is supple, he pats it into a ball, then carries it to the wet area of his shed.

On a potting wheel, a vase the height of a child stands drying. Beside it squats a smaller, rarely used wheel. With a thud, he throws the clay upon the rusty plate, sits to dip his hands in water, then cups them around the mound and softly presses the pedal. Leaning over the spinning mass, the potter pushes the sides as ropes of slurry dribble over his knuckles. Gradually the clay yields to his will as it centres on the spinning plate. He re-wets his hands. Then drives his thumbs into the centre and pulls out and up as a bowl takes shape. Repeatedly, his fingers draw the clay upwards until he curves the lip of the bowl with fingers poised like pistols. The wheel comes to a stop as the potter wipes his hands and slices his creation from its peak with piano wire. It's placed upon a wooden tray. Twice more he forms from the same wedge of clay until three wet bowls sit side by side on the board. As he rises from his stool, an antique dog shuffles into the shed to the sound of rain on the tin roof. The potter asks her a question as he picks up the bag the sad woman had left him. Understanding the intent, if not his words, his old friend follows him to the glazing room.

The next day, when leather dry, the potter turns the bowl's bases to square ridges so they will sit flat upon a table. Underneath, in the centre of each, he presses his wooden seal, leaving behind an indented capital P. On the fourth day, he fires the bowls along with thirty other pieces of assorted sizes and intended use. On the sixth day, the bowls are glazed and baked in a hotter kiln. This time, he fires them on their own.

I watch the potter lift a bowl from the box lined with wood shavings. His powerful hands are soft from a morning spent in water.

"It's beautiful!" I say, running my fingers across the dark blue surface. Trapped in the perfect glass, a star-filled galaxy shines up at me.

"Those golden flecks are from that dust you gave me," he says with arms folded across his chest.

The flecks feel warm.

"They're handsome bowls. What do I owe you?"

Now is the potter's turn to study me. I feel his attention as I continue to slide my fingers across the surface.

"It's a colour I haven't seen before," he says.

I know he wants me to look at him. He can tell I'm blinking quickly.

The potter softly says, "I'll swap them for more dust."

My hand stops moving, and I look up into those searching eyes.

"I'm sorry, that's all there was."

With a faint nod, he hands me the box with the other bowls wrapped in paper. "If that's the case, then they're a gift."

On the kitchen bench, vegetables from our garden sit in a row. An onion, carrots, celery sticks, potatoes, and a swede. With the largest knife and heaviest board, I peel and chop until the pot is full, then add stock, herbs, and barley. Lunch takes an hour to cook.

Out the window, across the lawn, stands the apple tree we planted forty years ago. Its aging branches shade a round picnic table that was a wedding gift from my parents.

Peter appears at my side. "Here, let me carry that."

My boy takes the tray with its tureen and blue bowls. He has thin hands, not like his father's.

"I've made too much soup," I say, then add under my breath, "again."

I let Peter lead us across the lawn to the waiting table.

"Just freeze it for later. It'll keep," he says.

As we walk, the air is still and smells of cut grass. I hear spoons clatter on the tray held out before him.

"Are these bowls new? They're the same colour as Dad's delphiniums."

I'm pleased he sees the likeness.

It's quiet today; the cicadas are resting. Replaced by a hum of my bees as they collect nectar and pollen from the flowers in the garden. Beneath the apple tree, Lisa is reading her father's old copy of *Mrs Dalloway*. She closes it as Peter lowers the tray to the table.

"Gosh, these are pretty!" Lisa turns a bowl around in her hands.

"Don't you think they look just like Dad's flowers?" Peter says.

Lisa agrees and sets the bowls before us on the grey weathered timber. I'm glad she remembered to bring cushions from the verandah, these outdoor chairs are becoming awfully hard on my back. Peter offers to serve and opens the tureen. Cooked vegetables mask the smell of the lawn.

"What do you think, Mum?" Peter asks. "We were talking before and I said we should go to the ocean, but Lisa says it's better to stay here in the garden."

I watch as he scoops into the soup.

"What would you like? It's your choice, of course."

For a moment, the ladle floats above my bowl, then the stars vanish as the soup covers them.

"Hmm?"

I feel Lisa's hand on mine. When I turn to face her, I see her father's eyes.

"Peter and I were wondering, Mum. What would you like to do with Dad's ashes?"

To The Sun

Irina Frolova

somewhere on the way the feathers
                    got burnt
scattered
                    a no-longer wife
a prodigal daughter
          a lost mother
you lie
                    on one side of the bed
you love
                    sinking into the small hours
          the silence of it
calling to
                    the oblivion
the memories
          the ghosts
                    take it all
light breaks
                    through the gaps
          the paradox
rays stretch
                    the shadows
embrace
          a new day

SECTION 3

NOT SO OLD ...

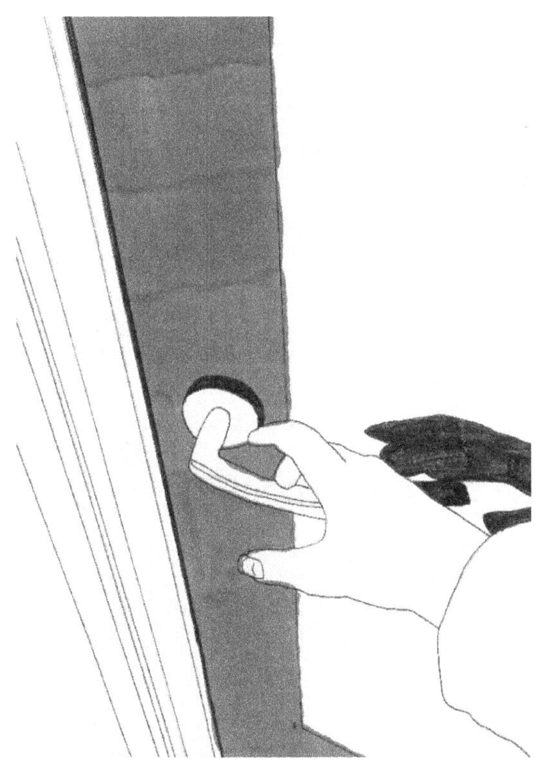

Levisia

Gurgica Georgina Chakar

A few days before I moved into my new home, I received a message from the previous tenants that my neighbour, Levisia Sanders, was going to sue me. We have owned this house for many years, but now *I* will live in it for the first time. It is no longer *we*. I have known Levisia for just as long. We share a love of art. She rose to the top of the Australian elite. I turned to the desire and belief in myself that I would succeed if I had at least five dollars in my pocket to buy more canvases and paints. But I didn't have them.

Levisia and I are separated by a thin wooden fence with a poorly attached gate, and a narrow path that she claimed as her own. In front of the fence in my yard is a eucalyptus tree that is several decades old. It was time to trim the branches. They grew far above the yards of the neighbours and over the fence with Levisia. In the past, through the gap between the gate and the fence, I have often seen her take out empty bottles and throw them into the recycling bin. Later I found out from the neighbours these were empty wine bottles. *Artists are sometimes better motivated after a glass or two,* I thought to myself. That was over ten years ago. Now I noticed that she had replaced the garbage bins with large flowerpots. Levisia Sanders is going to sue me?! The same

Levisia who once freed me from the shadow of my artistic frustrations, will sue me?!

"G," my tenant called me on the phone. "Levisia sent us an invitation for her retrospective exhibition. It's being held at Sydney University. She emphasised your presence as very dear." Levisia saw my daughter less often these days. That's why I wasn't surprised that she sent the invitation to my tenant who was a close friend of my daughter's. They lived together in our house while I spent my life on two, sometimes three continents.

A few days after I spoke to my tenant, I personally received a handwritten invitation from Levisia, which read, *"My dear, I think of you more often. See you at the exhibition. Yours L."* The exhibition would be held just days before I flew west from Australia again. That was five or six years ago.

When I go to exhibitions, I have no expectations. I always read about the artist, however I let the event surprise me with the exhibits, with the ambience of the space, with the visitors. These attendees are especially interesting to me. Do some of them come to be seen standing in groups with a glass of champagne where everyone is talking and no one is listening, or to see the exhibits?

At Levisia Sanders' exhibition, a group of men and women gathered in a circle in the middle of the hall were talking heatedly about the past. I moved slowly between them, managing to hear a few sentences. With champagne in one hand and a canape in the other, they evoked memories from decades of creative life, theirs and that of Levisia.

"Our tyre blew in the middle of nowhere. You remember?!!" The famous miniaturist laughed loudly with his head tilted back, as if he was talking to the ceiling. "The van was full of canvases."

"I told you to arrange an art courier," said the man in a vivid colourful shirt.

"No way! We would have missed the chance for the cows to see our exhibits. Their critique was worth its weight in gold. Haha ka ka kaaa," the miniaturist laughed. "And you, my dear, received an award for a national work in the Parliament, do you remember?"

"Yes, yes." She remembered lugging their art to Canberra for the anniversary celebration of the opening of the new parliament.

"Hahaha. The cow peeked through the windows of the van. Moo, moo, moo." She tried to smile again, but her voice lost confidence.

"Levisia, laugh less. The doctor ..." Her assistant next to whom I was standing with my glass of champagne, short on her toes, spoke softly into her neck. Levisia flinched as if to avoid her presence. I heard gossip in the neighbourhood that the two of them were lesbians. That she not only did her secretarial work but slept in the 'brickyard' two nights a week. That's what I called the huge brick warehouse in which my neighbour lived across the thin wooden fence and the path decorated with her pots and flowers.

"She got the warehouse as part of the divorce." Obviously, my tenant knew the neighbourhood well. "Wet and smelly," she explained with a grimace of disgust. Probably with the same grimace on her face she tells the neighbours that I also got this house as part of my divorce.

The camaraderie among the visitors of this exhibition seemed to be reaching a climax. It was time for honourable speeches from several of the attendees, who gave them without sparing the words exalting her artistic talent.

As they spoke, I could feel Levisia's gaze on my face. I recognised the same look she gave me when, a few years ago, she promised me she would influence the NSW artists' association to get me an exhibition space for free, and more importantly to get me sponsors and media exposure. That day she gave me one of her paintings. "The sun has changed course, my dear. Now it's shining on your face." Handing the painting to me, she added, "You might need it if one day the last five dollars slips out of your pocket."

"G, you lingered on each picture for a long time." Elena rarely addressed me by my full name. She called me only G. Many in our living circle adopted her speech. “We are waiting for your comment on the exhibition.”

Sitting next to her fiancé who drove us all to the exhibition, my daughter pinched his ear, a gesture she used to make with me when she was a child. “Hey sweetheart, didn’t I tell you that Levisia only drinks white wine. Why did you give her a red one?” she asked her fiancé.

The chance to give my opinion of the exhibition lost momentum.

The move to the new home created a big mess of packaging and furniture, and equipment that could not be installed because the handymen were still renovating my bathroom and laundry. Large pieces of furniture did not enter through the main entry door. Never having been replaced, the old English door led to a narrow corridor with high ceiling and heritage cornices. The only option was the path between the thin wooden fence and the ‘brickyard’.

I needed the key to the back gate, which only she had. The tenant in my house did not have a key. She was a big woman. She told me she couldn’t drag the garbage bins down the footpath because the concrete was broken into several pieces. That a while ago Levisia tripped on the concrete, fell and broke her wrist. She was afraid that she may get hurt on the broken footpath as well. That’s why she didn’t need the key. She kept the bins on the veranda in front of the house.

"*I* already solved the problem with the footpath. Remember? The concrete is not broken any more."

My tenant remained deaf to my comment.

"Tomorrow at noon I'm meeting the neighbour across the footpath," I told Elena.

"Levisia? Great. Don't go empty handed."

I wanted to buy a bouquet of flowers. Instead, I bought a box of chocolates. I remembered the bouquet that I gave her at her retrospective exhibition five or six years ago held at Sydney Uni. She held the flowers for a few moments on her chest, lying on top of her long, white hair that flowed freely over her shoulders. Slim and tall, dressed in a velvet dress, she looked even more beautiful than in the pictures on the internet.

"Knock … harder at the gate. The doorbell … doesn't work …" said Levisia on the phone. So I did. With the chocolate box in the decorative paper bag, I stood in front of the gate of the big warehouse until I was let inside.

A slightly hunchbacked woman with short, greying hair opened the gate for me. On her feet she wore slippers which, just like their name, she dragged on the travertine tiles, failing to raise her feet at least a little to take steps. She was saying something to me as she approached the front door. But her voice was so deep and muted that I barely managed to understand a word or two. She squeezed the doorknob several times, until finally the front door of the house opened. Her fingers were shaking, weak. I had enough time to notice that the garden was neat and well maintained. The goldfish, obviously well fed, were swimming in clear water.

"The fish seem safe from cats, birds ..." While I was talking, I felt a lump in my throat. It started choking me. Without an answer to my question, I continued to follow the pace set by the old woman.

A tall space appeared in front of me, covered with a glass roof. A space in which I felt inside as much as I was outside, under a clear sky. It was paved with travertine tiles, the same as those in the courtyard. The pots were like the ones outside on the footpath, and the flowers healthy and green from regular watering. The upper floor was a gallery that ran along the surrounding walls. From it, you enter rooms on three sides, and from the fourth you step out onto an open space housing the swimming pool.

I stood in the middle of the open room with a look of astonishment, my eyes darting to take in the entire space. The brickyard was a palace. A large painting by Levisia Sanders hung on each wall. I remembered them all because I saw them at the retrospective exhibition. "They look like two different styles." I made the comment at the time. It was on my lips again, during my visit to the warehouse, worthy of an artist of Levisia's profile. Then she told me that she worked for a long time to be able to change her painting style.

Now I got no answer from this thin, weak woman. I tried to swallow the lump in my throat, or at least expel it. But it was stronger than me. It became firmer when I once again looked at my famous neighbour, this time in her jeans, tight and worn. I sat on the dining chair opposite her. I noticed that on her left hand she was wearing the same gold bracelet that she had worn at the exhibition.

"I must not wear … anything on my right hand. My skin is thin and vulnerable."

I looked at the hand with the thin skin and remained silent.

"They took out … a piece of it and … planted it in my throat. Cancer … it was close to being fatal."

"I'm glad you beat the cancer, Levisia," I said after a short pause. The lump in my throat would not leave me. I sat and listened to the barely recognisable words of my host. I noticed that she told me several times the story of her dog that ate one of her very expensive shoes that she wore to receptions and parties.

She showed me a picture of the dog and made me tea. Then she sat back on the chair with an empty look in her eyes, not saying a word for a while. I drank the tea and made a small gesture as if I was getting up.

"My assistant … will walk you out. She will give you the key … to make a copy." She didn't move a bit. "Thanks for the chocolates." Then she immediately added, "I'm sorry, what … was your name?"

"Gina." Already standing up in front of her, I hastened to ask her about what I went for, in addition to asking for a copy of the key. "Levisia, if there is a neighbourhood problem that I need to solve, feel free to tell me."

"There's no problem." She coughed a little. "Yes, you … are Gina." She lifted her eyelids with difficulty to look at me once more. "The sun has changed its course, my dear. It's still on yours … but not in my face … no. Now … in the mirror I see …" She coughed again. At that moment I felt like hugging her, hugging Levisia Sanders.

Her assistant looked just as beautiful as at the exhibition. "Stay longer if you want to view the paintings."

"I saw them at the exhibition six years ago." The words slowly escaped my parched lips.

"I know, I remember you. You were the only one who brought her a bouquet of flowers."

I looked at the assistant curiously.

"Then you took a picture of her with your daughter and her fiancé."

I wanted to say a lot more to Levisia's assistant. Instead, I choked. I wanted to tell her how much I blame the empty bottles of … the paints and the brushes that drained the best from her. Long nights working on each painting, then exposing it to the world for their two or three minute observation.

Instead, I asked her what her favourite book was.

"The portrait of Dorian Gray," she answered without a second thought.

It took me a few more steps to get out of the gate onto the sidewalk when I remembered something very important. I turned to Levisia's assistant ready to speak. She pre-empted me. "My dear, Levisia does not step on an ant. Her kindness will not allow her to take you to court." I noticed her slowly closing the gate. "Sometimes in my absence she drinks white wine, contrary to the doctor's orders. Then she mourns the past." She shook her head a little. "She mourns for the power to take the world in her hands." She licked her lips. "Then the wine threatens to sue the neighbours, me, and she herself suffers the most." The gate almost closed. I heard the assistant uttering the last words. "By the way, you solved the problem with the broken concrete on the footpath a few years ago, remember? Have a nice day, my dear."

Break in

Bronwyn MacRitchie

I turn to catch the breeze on my face. Stale cigarette smoke blended with orange blossoms wafts in. Footsteps shuffle past. They stop outside my bedroom window. My eyes spring open. It's dark. Pitch dark.

A goods train rumbles across the valley. The wheels scratch and the sound of rumbling wagons ricochets around the surrounding hills, camouflaging this unfamiliar disturbance. I lay still. Listen. Senses so alert I can hear the rustling wings of the doves in the trees outside.

A car door slams. When the footsteps continue down the side path, towards the back, my heartbeat increases. Every hair on my arms is a tuning fork.

Damn. I should have replaced those solar lights when I came home from my trip yesterday. The car is being serviced, so the carport is empty. Do they think no-one's home? The footsteps return. I freeze when the window screen clinks. His breath exhales a faint wheeze as fingers slide down the frame searching for the clips. I try to swallow, but my mouth is dry.

I wriggle across the bed and slide to the floor with as much stealth as my raspy doona will allow. Should I evade or defend? I reach for the cricket bat but realise I could go to jail for assault. Escape? Back door: noisy bolt. Front door: dead lock.

I squat on the floor. My knees don't like this position. I stopped doing squats when I turned seventy last year. When the ancient window slides open in slow, jerky increments, it's time to move. The curtain rustles.

Hide. I need to hide, but where? Bed's too low; wardrobes are jammed with junk. Think, girl, think! I crawl along the floor into the living room. On the way, my knee crushes what I hope is a peanut and not a cockroach. Paranoia at every tiny sound keeps me alert.

The baby grand piano in the corner. Underneath, amongst my gig equipment, is refuge. I'm almost there when the muffled rustle of cloth drags across the window ledge followed by a faint thump on the carpet. *Good grief, he's inside.*

I creep beneath the piano, cautious about bumping my head, which happens each time I'm rummaging under there. There's not much room. An old bedspread, used as my piano cover, dangles in odd triangles over the sides. Perhaps camouflage from the intruder.

I grope past the bits of equipment and squeeze behind the piano pedals. Fine particles settle on my face. Must've been a while since I cleaned under here. My nose tingles. *Don't sneeze.*

It's taken a moment for my eyes to adapt. Feet cast a shadowy outline as soft footfalls inch across the carpet. Slight vibrations reach me. The fridge gurgles and quiets. He pauses but the draught from his movement reaches me. I hug my knees and stifle my breathing, aware that the closeness of guitar strings could be a disaster if I move. The room is compact and small. I know the pathways between each piece of furniture from frequent night visits to the toilet. Through my mental layout of the room, I trace his movements.

Damn. My craft and computer are in the back room. Is this someone I know? Do they know the house?

When he jabs his toe on the corner of the couch there's a sharp intake of breath. Good, I hope he bangs his head on the cabinet. His toe cracks as he sneaks across the carpet. In the stillness it sounds like a gun shot.

I think of all the information stored on my computer. *Did I back up yesterday? Did I change the password? The headphones, the microphone? Will he take them all?* I've never had a break-in before. I clench my jaw to stop the rising panic.

He mutters a curse as a body part catches the edge of the keyboard on the piano. I hear faint taps along the wall as he traces his way towards the kitchen. Car lights flash past the front window. There's a glint of steel reflected in the glass cabinet door. *Oh hell. He's got a knife.*

Did I tell my children I loved them when last we spoke? I should have a dog. A big, black one with …

Then a crash on the lower keys of the piano shatters my hearing. It's deafening. I shriek. My head bangs the soundboard as my right foot bumps the guitar into the amplifier. He's kicked the leg of the piano stool and tripped onto the piano. I'd failed to close the lid and push the stool in after my last practice.

"Shit!" he utters. "Bloody hell …"

I clamp my hand over my mouth, stiffen and listen. His outline is clearer. I try to reach my cramped calf to give it a rub and look up. He's staring straight at me. I pant through my mouth as the odour of stale breath, musty clothes and cigarettes hits me.

He swears and jolts upright as the theme from *Goldfinger* blares out from his jacket.

I'm so startled I bang my head again. I'm expecting him to reach under the piano and drag me out.

Can't he see me! Didn't he hear me before? He must be deaf. All pretence of stealth evaporates as he attempts to extract the ringing phone.

"Shit, shit, bloody shit." His voice is no longer a whisper and the shadow dance towards the kitchen is comical and entertaining.

While he is distracted searching for his mobile, I begin to inch my way out from under the piano.

"Hello?"

I stop to listen. His wheeze is faint, but in the silence of my living room it's a squeaky door.

"Okay, okay. This place has junk everywhere."

I'm offended by his remark. There's not much room. Besides, antiques are not junk. It's a shame he's not on speaker, because I'm curious about who is on the other end of the phone.

"I know. In the back room. I'm heading there now."

He's moving towards the kitchen. If he's not careful …

The sudden slap of his bare feet on the linoleum in the kitchen forces me to retreat under the piano. Expletives follow a loud smack. The mobile flies out of his hand and illuminates a pathway to plop on the floor beside the piano stool. Fridge magnets descend like pellets on paper. The fridge rattles and protests with a few pops and gurgles.

A tinny voice from the mobile says "Greg?" The light dies, but I now know the name of my intruder.

Groans follow, then … nothing. I wait for a moan or whimper. Silence. I listen until my heart resumes its normal rhythm. Easing my way out from under the piano I sit and listen again.

Do I switch on the light, check if he's okay? Escape through the open window and phone the police?

I debate the possibilities when the scratch of a key being inserted into the front door lock chills my body. I tremble in dread of what may come. The front door opens with the scrape of swollen wood across the tiles. Another neglected chore.

With a click the lounge room is flooded in light and I need to shield my eyes from the glare. I risk a peek from beneath my hiding place.

"Toby, thank goodness." My grandson stands beside the door with a stunned expression. In my immense relief, tears well and limbs shake. I crawl out and clutch him. I'd given my daughter spare keys to the house while I was overseas for a month. However, I was confused. Why would he be checking on my place at this hour?

"Gran? What's wrong? I thought you were coming back on the weekend."

"Toby ..."

We turn together as moans from the kitchen floor reach us. Greg's eyes are open, his face distorts in pain. The wheeze is distinct with each short breath. Toby strides towards him.

"Toby mate. I think I've broken my leg."

"You know this man?" I'm appalled.

"You forgot the step." Greg's face contorts and with eyes squeezed tight — he is in obvious pain — he abandons movement and slumps back down.

"You know this person who broke into my home?" How could this be? "Why, Toby?"

He raises his arm, then drops it and I flinch as if he's slapped me.

"You weren't supposed to be here. But you came home early and messed up my plans."

"Plans? What plans?"

"Keys weren't in the meter box," Greg mutters.

I bend down and check his pulse, choosing to deal with Greg rather than wonder about my grandson's dubious nocturnal activities.

"His pulse is racing, Toby. He needs medical attention," I say. "He doesn't look good."

"Sorry Mrs M, I didn't mean to scare you," says Greg, eyes drooping and breathing shallow.

"That's okay," I pat his shoulder. "I'm feeling much better. Hang on. You know me?" This is getting weird.

"Yeah. Toby talks about you all the time."

"You seem a nice young man," I take hold of his hand. "How did you get mixed up in … this?"

"This?" says Toby. "Gran, it's not … Anyway, why are you home a week early?"

"Flight issues. I had to …" A loud knock on the door interrupts my explanation.

"Who on earth could that be?" I sit on the piano stool no longer afraid. I am indignant.

Toby strides over and when he opens the door, the muted, grey dawn behind three men indicates how advanced the time is.

"Here on time," says the tall, bearded redhead.

"Toby, what's going on? Why are these men here?" I turn to the three strangers standing outside my house. "Why are you here?"

"Jeeze, mate what happened to you?" Redhead pushes past Toby and me, followed by the other two. They squat down in front of Greg whose freckles are prominent against his pale skin.

The kitchen is crowded with bearded men in overalls.

"Tools … step … keys." Beads of sweat line Greg's brow. He's shivering.

"Somebody, call an ambulance," I say, and head towards the back room.

"Where are you going?" asks Toby.

"To get a blanket."

"I'll get it!" he says, overtaking me in two strides, returning a moment later with a blanket. He lays it across Greg. The men are silent, staring at me.

"I've phoned for an ambulance, Mrs M," says Redhead, "Be as quick as they can, they said."

"Thanks, er ..." I realise I don't know his name. "You know me too?" They all nod. This is bizarre. I smell subterfuge.

"Toby. Why don't you tell me what's going on? Please."

I'm interrupted by several loud knocks on the front door. This time it's three ambulance personnel with a stretcher.

"That was quick," says Redhead.

"Ambulance station is a few streets away," I say.

"What happened?" asks one of them as they weave around the various pieces of furniture to get to the kitchen. The stretcher is placed against the wall due to the lack of space.

I'm about to offer a brief explanation when Toby says pointing, "He tripped on the step and landed there."

A murmur of agreement from Greg and the others is accompanied by exchanged glances and copious nods.

"Okay. Let's see to the patient then," says another uniform.

The bearded men shift into the lounge room with Toby and sit on the couch. There is an uncomfortable silence between them as the team in the kitchen attend to Greg with swift efficiency. They load him on to the stretcher and depart through the back door, which leads off the kitchen.

"We'll follow," says Redhead. "Call you when we know the results, Toby. Thanks, Mrs M."

"What a disaster," says Toby, closing the door to a day promising to be warm.

I turn the light switch off. "Toby. Care to explain?"

"Greg left some of his tools here. He had an early job this morning."

"Tools?"

"We had to get to the floor safe."

"Oh, Toby. You only had to ask. I could've told you there's no money in there."

"Gran, it's not like that at all."

"What's that?" I asked, bending to retrieve an item poking out from beneath the fridge.

"It's a torch," says Toby. "Must be Greg's."

"Silver. I thought he had a knife." I flicked to the *on* position. "Flat batteries. I really thought he had a knife."

I felt foolish and relieved at the same time. "I hope he's going to be okay."

"The guys were working for me, Gran."

I hesitate, uncertain I'm ready for explanations.

“They’re builders. While you were on holiday, it was the perfect opportunity to get it done.”

“What done, Toby?”

“All the family chipped in. Everybody was sworn to secrecy.”

“Toby, what are you talking about?”

He extended his hand. “Let me show you.”

When he opened the back room door, I was stunned.

“It’s not finished yet. Cleaning up, mostly. A few finishing touches here and there.”

Gone was the dingy, dark room. Shelves lined the walls. A solid work table in the centre and a built in desk in the far corner still provided ample space for movement. Soft morning light streamed in through wide, glass doors that led to a deck beyond.

“It was to be a surprise. Big unveiling and all that. Had to move the safe to get the doors in. We discovered it from underneath.”

“Grandad did a good job of concealing it.” I chuckled at the thought. “It’s got the deeds to the house and my will, nothing else.”

“I know you always wanted a deck and a craft room with loads of natural light. Happy 70th, Gran.”

Ashmore Prophets

David Kelly

Their faces are crinkled, brown as cracked varnish
on marked-down op-shop wardrobes.

They come in arks that are throbbing and fumy
and in their heads carry their old believing.

And we fear them don't we? We resent even
that the sea — our sea — parts for these people.

And when they get here beseeching alms
and bread and meat from our strong kind navy

and they tread at last on the soil of our wide country,
washed, fed, lean, survivor proud though ragged

having come from lands burned-out bombed-out
but dry like ours, as old as ours, bone-sere, windy,

do we fear them not for the knives we think they carry
nor a future plague of Midwich Cuckoo children:

but that behind their eyes is something much older
than lies behind ours, far more multi-layered,

a hunger more at ease with the wispy breath of spirit,
something our ground-down deserts will welcome,

leading them with their rags and ranting lore
to the lost reefs that we've stopped searching for.

Grandad

Anne Andrews

Young Jim pushed hard on the pedals of his mountain bike up the last hill before Grandad's place, past the house and container sheds towards the rainforest that signified a big back paddock.

He waited at the entrance to catch his breath, but more so to listen for the sound of bellbirds. He heard instead the whoop-whoop of a swamp pheasant in the distance, and a raucous kookaburra spreading his joy, but also the warning of possible rain. No bellbird, though he remembered how excited he was to see his first koala in the big eucalypt that hung over the gate — a teenager like himself, cast adrift into the world and wondering what life was all about.

He coasted down the hill past autumn trees in bright colour and shedding their leaves. He parked his bike on the turning pad, skipped across some crazy paving, and knocked on the back door.

Grandad was as deaf as a post, but Jim wondered why the dogs hadn't made a cacophony of noise first.

He mosied on around the tiny cottage to the front deck, where four dogs greeted him with fear and love. Grandad stumbled out of his chair and almost fell. The dogs licked Jim and bounced off him in sheer delight. They were old and deaf like their owner!

"How are you, you young rascal?" he said as he swung the gate open.

"I'm well thank you, Grandad. How are you?" he answered politely, knowing that his grandfather had temporarily forgotten his name due to the demon dementia.

"I'm fit to burst!" old Jock replied, beating his bony chest with fists of gnarled fingers. "Why are you here? Has somebody died?"

"No, no. Not since Grandma, two years ago. Remember?"

"Not really, but there was a bit of a fuss sometime in the not-too-distant past."

Jim decided to let that one go, and continued, "I'm here to talk to you about your childhood – actually your teenage years."

"Oh, goodness, yes. I can remember it like yesterday, all hormones and honeybees."

Jim blushed; he knew he'd come to the right person.

Jock continued, "What d'you want to know?"

Jim shuffled, and very nearly lost his nerve, but blurted out anyway, "Girls! How d'you get to know and understand them?"

A cheeky smile cracked across Jock's face, and he stared off into the distance for a while. The view from the deck was indeed beautiful, and Jim would have liked to relax and enjoy it, but he needed to know something, anything, about love. Finally, Jock replied,

"Ah! Honeybees! You keep the Queen bee satisfied, that's all!"

Jim couldn't believe that Grandad got so straight to the point, and turned away quickly, grasping the deck rail as he remembered his wet dream the night before.

"Oh, okay, then tell me about your first girlfriend, will you Grandad?"

Jock turned abruptly towards his grandson and asked, "Firstly, how old are you?"

"F-fourteen," Jim replied, flustered, wishing he were twenty-four.

"Close enough, I was sixteen when I fell in love. She was everything a man could wish for, all tits and bum and a pretty face too! Forgot her name for the moment, but it'll come back later."

Jim made sure his grandfather was settled back into his wicker chair with lots of cushions and drew another chair close by. The dogs had given up on their quest for the longest pat, and lounged around them, soaking up bright morning sun as it cascaded through blue gums and spotted gums and the occasional smooth-barked apple. A peewee came to perch on the stair rail and watched on, intently.

"She was the talk of the town, about twenty-something and extremely popular with all the footballers. I used to hang about outside the pub in the hope of a lemonade, and one night she turned up in an old Packard."

Jim gave his grandfather time enough to settle his thoughts, waiting breathlessly for the next episode.

"She said 'G'day gorgeous' and fluttered her eyelashes at me, and my legs turned to jelly. Another part of my anatomy did just the opposite, so I had to turn away and face the wall."

Jock reminisced a little more, and Jim ached to hear the rest.

"Not a good start to a relationship, but more was to come. She laughed hilariously at me on that first occasion, and I thought I'd seen the last of her, with all those blokes indoors, waiting for her."

Jim could hardly sit still; his heart was racing, and his mouth was dry.

"The crowd inside the pub suddenly got raucous, and a fight broke out. She — I'll call her Doreen – came running out with her skirts and petticoats raised, showing knees of creamy white topped with red garters." Jock shifted in his chair before continuing, "She grabbed my hand and dragged me towards the Packard, asking if I could drive. I said, 'Yes' and she pushed me into the driver's seat, then got into the back seat saying she was too upset to drive."

He smiled. "I was in Seventh Heaven, with a beautiful old number to drive and a damsel in distress in the back seat! She told me, 'Take me to the Lookout, will you?' I don't know whether I sped or not, but we certainly got there pronto! I got out, cooling my heels, with anything but the magical lights of the town on my mind, and opened the back door to invite her to join me. 'Being a gentleman, you see,'" he added with a twinkle in his eye.

"She dragged me into the back seat. 'Come here gorgeous, but be careful with my hatbox,' she said. There was indeed a hatbox on the far side of the seat, and there it sat for the whole time I was there. Wasn't game to touch it!"

Jim was not prepared for this diversion to proceedings, and said gruffly, "C'mon Grandad, what happened next?"

"Well, I learned how to ride a bike, and I learned how to ride a bull, and I learned how to ride a horse, all at the same time!" Jim groaned, and Jock laughed at his grandson's impatience.

"That's what you've gotta get rid of, young Jim, your impatience! Take it slow and talk a lot. Don't know whether she remembered me for my pace, or my conversation, or for the fact that I never disturbed her precious bloomin' hatbox, but we kept on meeting on a regular basis."

"But Grandad, she was ten years older than you, and there must have been a lot of gossip going on."

"There certainly was, but we took to meeting up on rural roads, out of sight, very circumspect."

"How long did this go on for, Grandad?"

"At least five years, and as soon as I turned twenty-one, I proposed."

"But Grandad, surely the family disapproved, and there were plenty of other men she could have married."

"Well Jim, I saw the other side of the dear girl — the vulnerable hurt child in her — and you must do the same. Always look for the good in people and be a kind person yourself."

"Was it all smooth sailing, or did you have any problems along the way?"

"There was one occasion when the whole countryside had been inundated with record rain. I was working in a dairy about thirty kilometres out of town, and a ditch opened up in the access road. I had no way of letting Doreen know, as there were no mobile phones then, so she drove on out blithely one night and crashed down twenty metres where the road had been washed away."

"Was she hurt? How did you find out? Where is the car now?"

"Slow down, boy, one question at a time! She suffered a few broken bones and was knocked unconscious. I'd finished milking for the day, and this pesky peewee kept darting at me from the bail gate. I sensed something was wrong, so I drove slowly towards town in the farm ute."

"Go on. How come you didn't crash too?"

"I used low beam, and a spotlight attached to the roof. I soon noticed several trees on the edge of the road standing at odd angles and occasionally shuddering, so I stopped and walked the last few metres with my torch and a hand-held two-way. You wouldn't believe the immensity of that landslide! Sickening it was, but I still scarpered down the rock face and found her alive, thank goodness."

"Hurry up! What happened next?"

"I rang triple zero and organised an ambulance, then called my boss at the dairy and requested help. I simply cradled her in my arms until someone arrived. Good thing I left the warning lights flashing on the ute, even if it flattened the battery. Both the ambulance and my boss arrived simultaneously, and we soon had her winched up and taken to hospital."

"I'll bet the rumours circulated after that!"

"Yes, and all of them unkind. The members of the football club were the worst gossips — said she was randy and drunk! I just held my tongue and never let on that it was me she was driving to see that night."

"So, where's the old car now, Grandad?"

"Just over the hill there," Jock pointed behind him. Council never fixed the road, and the hole is overgrown with weeds and saplings. Used to be a tourist attraction, but now it's just a thing of the past."

"I might go and have a look for curiosity's sake, if you don't mind?"

"Yes, of course, but be careful on the loosened scree."

Jim rode across the bumpy tracks on Grandad's farm to a gate he knew was always unlocked, past the rainforest and onto the neighbour's place. He finally got to hear the bellbirds he loved when he first set foot on the farm. Their scintillating songs fell on his ears, plaintively, echoing his own yearnings. The neighbours were absent, so he quickly rode over the airstrip and along a short track to their entrance on the main road. He saw cement barriers just past their gate. It was easy to squeeze the bike through a narrow gap, and after a short walk, he came to the abyss.

"Holy Hell! What a hole!"

The same drunken trees that Grandad had talked about stood sentinel on the other side of the gap. A giant rockface some hundred metres long at a 45-degree angle, could be seen as the culprit in the carnage. Great chunks of tar and hundreds of dead trees, splintered like matchsticks, littered the slope for another five hundred metres downhill.

Jim also noted that everywhere there was an entanglement of young saplings, native hibiscus and honeysuckle, lantana, and tobacco bush.

Right in the middle, almost indistinguishable, was the old Packard in pieces! Jim parked his bike well back from the rim and scampered warily down a bit of a cow track, mostly on his bum and clutching at blady grass.

He went straight to a back door, open at a skewed angle and almost off its hinges, in search of his prize. There, on the partly unravelling back seat was a hatbox, undisturbed apart from the exigencies of occasional storms that lashed horizontally through any openings. It was mouldy on top, but a pattern of refined English ladies and Victorian advertisements could still be seen, faded under a brown leather trim.

"My goodness, it's still here after fifty years!"

He opened it up. There was a bonnet inside, which he gently lifted out. It was cream. The felted crown was still intact, with no mould to be seen. The short muslin veil was embroidered with hand-sewn spots, and a single white silk flower held everything in place. It was very modish, if that was the right word, thought Jim.

But something else, previously hidden by the bonnet, caught Jim's attention.

A fob watch on a chain winked at him, and at the same time, a peewee swooped down from the roof, pestering him, on its way to a nearby branch. He brushed the bird aside, and clasping the beautiful silver timepiece in his hand, he sat down on the back seat and prised the lid open. There was an inscription:

To the best lover in the World
To J. from D.
XX

Jim's mouth opened wide in astonishment. Instead of settling his confused notions, this opened a Pandora's box of new connotations.

He packed the watch and bonnet back into the hatbox and carried it gingerly and carefully up the slope.

With every step he took upwards, he slipped back three, but even one-handed as he was, he gradually gained ground, and eventually, the top.

He lay exhausted for about fifteen minutes, making sure the hatbox was safe, before tying it to the back of the bike with baling twine.

Meanwhile, another peewee, or perhaps it was the same one, kept dive-bombing him, egging him to return to Grandad's deck quick time.

Jim's legs didn't have to pump so hard on the trip back, as it was mostly downhill. This gave him time to cogitate, to ruminate, to run known facts through his mind, joining the dots together. He thought about the beautiful pattern etched into the silver casement of the watch — concentric lines criss-crossing delicately, and all leading to a heart in the middle, surrounded by flowers and leaves.

"Where is the heart of Grandad's story?" he called out to the surrounding forest. The bellbirds answered back in tones of joy.

"Why did I never ask Grandma about her life?" he continued, and the kookaburras responded in derision.

Jim shook his head as he opened the neighbour's gate, and cruised down the farm track, which had beautiful views ahead and dense rainforest beckoning on the right. He ignored both, and after a short uphill spurt, he saw the house and sheds sitting picturesquely above a small dam. Grandad and the suddenly noisy dogs were still soaking up sun on the deck.

Jim placed the hatbox in the shadows under the steps and extricated the fob watch. He mounted the stairs slowly, feeling reasonably happy that his small individual problems had been overcome, that the power of a love much greater than his own would soon be explained, that patience and kindness would become his greatest assets in the future.

"Aha, you're back safely! How'd you go mate?"

Jim lovingly placed the watch in Jock's hands and waited. Jock stared at the watch for several minutes before opening the lid, and then a tear fell down one grizzled old cheek, followed by others, unbeckoned.

"My goodness, I've been looking for that for an awfully long time. Your grandmother gave it to me on my twenty-first birthday. Where'd you find it?"

A peewee landed on the deck rail and sang delightedly. Jim reached down and picked up the hatbox and gave it to his grandfather, with reverence.

Grandad's smile said it all!

The Old Time Swing

Tom Williamson

Gus left his room at mid-morning and meandered out to the living room. He tightened the hold on his walking cane that limped along with him, his third limb to support his aching joints. His lips pressed tight together. There was nothing serious about walking down the hall, but there was nothing cheerful about it either.

He stopped in the kitchenette, across the hall from reclined people reading, sleeping and daydreaming. As he always did, he took a cup from the top drawer and a spoon from the bottom. He gave himself three teaspoons of instant and two of sugar. The kettle light flicked, and the bell dinged. The loudest noise in the village. Three-quarters the height of the cup in water and a quick stir, he almost had his mug.

Thank God for coffee.

Gus checked over his shoulder for a nurse and unhurriedly checked the other for good measure. No signs of a nurse. He unscrewed the handle on his walking stick and separated it from the body. He opened the latch at the tail of the handle and dispensed cheap Scotch into the last quarter of his cup.

Thank God for Scotch.

Old habits, like old soldiers … die hard.

The grooved pattern from daily use in his armchair took his frame gently once more. Just the same as it did yesterday and the way it will tomorrow. He took a sip from his drink and observed the room.

The jukebox across the room rested in almost sentimental silence. It was old and frail like the rest of the room's inhabitants, but it didn't demand much attention. It buzzed just below the hum of the dishwasher and the birds outside. It had an endearing crackle.

Martin murmured in his sleep. Eleanor whispered to Susie about her granddaughter's school play and Cynthia gave a young business lady a kiss on the cheek at the doorway.

The liquor in the coffee swirled on the back of his palate. Gus closed his eyes for a moment. He could hear a saxophone in the background. The lights of some unknown place seemingly blurred into one and spoke of a distant past. Bright red lights flashed across a blank canvas mind like streaks of blood upon a shield. Harmonic movements of vision superimposed upon a black background. A calamity of memory and a riot of sounds. There was dancing and there was laughter, but the faces of people morphed into one. Chatter buzzed past his peripherals, but his ears failed to get a grip on the words. The souls around him were breathing hard and their legs were thumping against wooden floors. The lights whirled again, and the natural ambience of the home took over as the opening of his eyes brought him back to his chair. The sax was gone, and the crackle of the speaker returned.

Her hair was tied up in a neat bun to match her matte black pants and blazer. Her teeth gleamed through a professional smile of red lipstick. She received frail waves and a crowd of friendly greetings from around the room.

"Anna my dear!" Cynthia said. "It's so good to see you," and she received a score of approving hums. Gus watched the business looking lady greet various folks in the home before making a direct path for him. She came and knelt beside his armchair.

"How are you doing, Oldie?" she said as she placed her smooth hand on his.

Gus retracted his arm the slightest bit and he felt a subtle chill of a stranger's touch sent a shiver to his bones. This didn't seem to bother her at all.

Who is this lady?

She began to speak of her day. How she was meeting a client for lunch and how she thought she would stop by the home on her way through. Still, like the morning thus far, his upper lip remained firm and thin.

Why is she telling me this?

She continued to speak about the mundane rituals of her job and the pressing matters at hand. Her eyes would read the confusion pouring out of his face, but her mouth would move on stoically without much hesitation. The sunlight that crept its way through the trees outside, swayed gently on the girl's face in accordance with the wind. The flickering light showed off the sapphire blue of her eyes.

Cynthia tinkered with the dial on the jukebox and soft applause of a live audience chirped in the corner. The next jazzy tune joined the hums of the nursing home.

Blasted music. Always so damn loud.

Gus' mind continued to drift between those red lights of the bar and the sleepy sunlight passing through the windows. The shouts of that crowd and the voice of the businesswoman seemed to have no boundary. An eclipse of reality and yesteryear.

The previous song ended, and Lil Hardin Armstrong began to crackle over the speakers. A new tune fluttered in the air and it induced finger snaps and foot stamps in the musically inclined.

"You remember this one then, Grumpy." The lady by his side looked up at him with a mysterious sense of glee. "Surely! Come on, Smiley," she joked.

To the surprise of the home, she stood up. She unclipped her barrette and let her hair down. The smart black shoes were left on the ground behind her as she walked towards the jukebox.

What is she doing?

Anna began to move with every second beat of the song. A soft sway, the way a sunflower would in light summer wind. Long brown hair rocked back and forth as her waist pulled from side to side. A half smile of contentment complemented her face as she danced alone in a space full of people. Cynthia turned the dial on the volume and the room's attention perked up.

Gus squinted his eyes. The red lights seemed to jolt in and out of his frame of vision. He clenched his eyes shut and laid his head back against the overused chair. The voice slowly became clearer and the red light moved from a blur to a neon sign. The wrinkled crow's feet under eyes tingled as the saxophone became apparent and drew him in further. The jazz was like a rope tied around his mind, it reeled him in until he saw *'Boston's Finest Tailor'* written boldly above the door.

He knew that, when entering, the door should always be closed behind you, and he did so.

The first thing he noticed as he walked down the iron stairs was that the air smelled of whiskey and appeared blue from cigarettes. The buzz of one hundred conversations each fought microcosmic battles with the music. The swinging rhythm moved as effortlessly as the smoke under the East Coast streets.

He led the way down into the sunken cacophony, her hand safe in his. Down below, the shoulders of returned soldiers rocked and their partners' heels tapped unconsciously in submission to the notes of the double bass. Notes with enough soul to reach heaven or wake the dead. Cheeks tingled when the jazz saxophone began. It soothed clenched jaws and ironed out irritated face lines.

Queues for the bar hopped in synchronisation. The bar where amber liqueur lined the wall in unmarked bottles. He felt lost in joy among the top hats that bounced and suit tails that fluttered as men free of war, moved with glee and illicit drinks in hand. He looked back to see Sadie's smile and her ocean-blue eyes wide with excitement. Rye whiskey cocktails shaken with the juice of the cheapest lemons and a tinge of egg whites served with a smile and bowtie. It was luxury of the most frugal kind. Masonry lined the walls and joined the roof in smooth curves with enough arc for Caesar himself to be jealous. Endless vectors for sound to bounce off.

The music cut. The crowd parted. Men took off their hats and removed their coats. Girl and boy stood parallel waiting for the beat. Her red dress sparkled in the dim bar lights and her red lipstick dazzled against the white of that smile. The double bass began. The trumpet returned and the piano joined the show. He leant forward, she grabbed his suspenders and they held their gaze, her honeyed breath caught his attention before she pushed him away and she spun like the jazz ballerina she was.

Their feet sprang to life. Infinite power to disperse through toes, knees and their hips. Eight count circular motions took the whole crowd. Each pair swept across the dancefloor, soaking up every inch of space but never colliding. The girls spun with limitless energy, electrons floating around their stable atoms. They improvised together in magnificent clarity, understanding each step and beat with one another. A blending of feet and young hands electrified their swing dance.

A shortness of breath and blood rushing like wildfire they recovered at the end of the song, Sadie's bluebell eyes glistened back at him among the red bar lights. His wife's hands in his and they danced into the night. Until they could no more.

Gus opened his eyes. Sat up in his chair and swigged the rest of his coffee. Oriental Swing and Lil Hardin's voice still sounded peacefully in the back of his ears. Anna still continued to dance on her own. He levered himself up. A straight back and his head high, he looked across at Anna still swaying in blissful contentment. No one looked at him stand, the room still half asleep. He loosened his grip and tossed the stick aside. It hit the floor with a dull thud. This awakened the room slightly. Eyes flashed in his direction. A pair of nurses watched on. They prepared to dash but they remained motionless with their mouths moderately ajar.

The first step without aid in a year. He hobbled on his left and caught his balance back on his right as a sailor does upon returning to land. In short shuffles, Gus ventured across the nursing home floor. The crackle of the speaker became more enticing as he approached. Agony invaded his back and the cartilage in his knees screamed for rest.

Anna had stopped dancing to witness this too. There was a dull slam as his hand slapped the oak speaker table. Shaky fingers extended to twist the volume dial even further and Lil Hardin's voice dominated the birdsong.

After a few more stumbles before he presented an inviting, outstretched hand. Her half smile turned full. Fingers interlocked and accepted the invitation. The song hit a slow point and the two moved to the left. The swing band got louder, and the pace quickened. A large loopy spin, Gus led the young lady around in a slow and melodic whirl. His bones creaked and his muscles tensed but their smiles dominated the home. Every piece of attention was seized as the dance provoked a contagious gaze.

Their slow swing stretched no more than a few square metres. Tears welled in the corner of Anna's eyes and she could see understanding beginning to dawn in his.

Stumbles stole some of his rhythm. She would fasten her grip and lock her joints to hold her Old Man up. Gus felt his forehead unfurrowing and his lips relaxing. She caught him as he tripped over his own toes and corrected his stance. Her tears were more prominent and his upper lip no longer stiff. His cheeks tingled the way they did that night in the bar at the sound of the saxophone and someone to dance with. Her blue eyes were most prominent when they swung back left, towards the table and into the near-midday sunlight. They were the same as Sadie's eyes that night. They were the same as Sadie's for the rest of their long marriage.

She has the same eyes as her mother.

For the first time in years, Anna saw him smile. His lips trembled, but his feet were strong. He smiled for the movement and the sound of the music.

He smiled at the remembrance of those eyes, her name and her smile. He smiled at the thought of the girl's mother.

He smiled at the chance to dance with his daughter.

You cannot separate a soldier from his drink
nor the bass from the band
nor a dancer from his dance.

SECTION 4

A GROWING THING ...

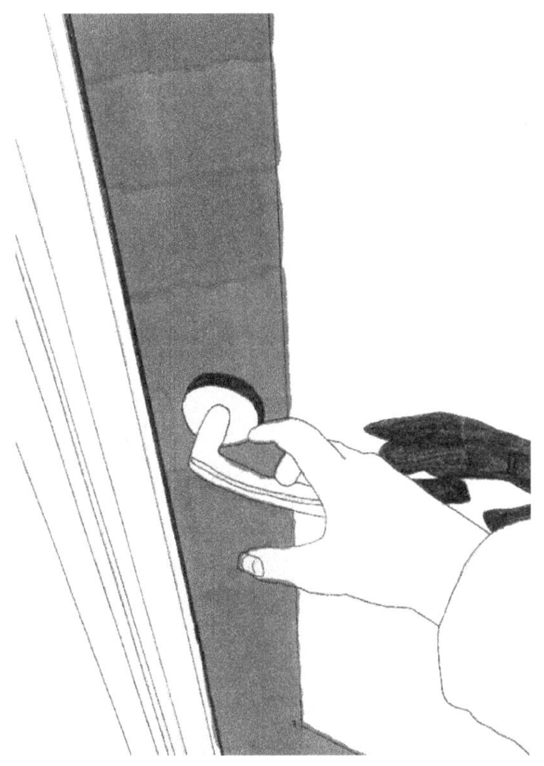

The Old Sand Mining Site

Kathryn Fry

This poem was awarded *Second Prize*
in the poetry category of the
Alice Sinclair Memorial Writing Competition.

Come into the garden. Honeyeaters lift
our eyes to the canopies and let them linger

on the wild canvas of lines and shades,
and how light paints the leaf-shifting spaces.

Blue wrens sketch a path over soil freed
of common couch and *commalina;* they loiter

by the *westringia* on their way. Nearby
wetlands harbour paperbarks and an open

sky above a wash of native bulrushes.
There's music in the silences of jewel beetles

(their blues and reds uncovered in the back bed)
or the rush of a brown spider or rainbow skink

across the earth, and the burst of scent as we
brush past mint bush. And in the undulations

of the black and yellow taileds lumbering away.
The fruits of midgen or apple berry may curb

a longing for taste but the nursery needs seeds
and cuttings today from *correa* and *boobialla.*

To bend, to tend to the garden and nursery
is to feel the weight of your shadow-self

evaporate, as if being in no time. Imagine
years of readying the many for bush renewal

or urban, the stories in everything endemic
from the ground up. This is a place for the heart,

head and hands, they say. Belonging thrives
here, lively as a fantail at the bird bath. Come

among the birdsong and bonhomie with those
sowing or pricking out for stock. And sometime

take your time to wander in the large shade house
on this old sand mining site off Kalaroo Road

to stop before the rows of young gums, and
take in their hues, habits and dazzling vigour.

The Sign

Allan Nicholls

I remember that day in '69 like it was yesterday. My marble was drawn from the barrel and I was conscripted into the army. I hadn't exactly been looking forward to it, but I'd told myself, if my number came up I was going to do nasho. Not that it was a big decision. The alternative was jail as a conscientious objector.

I was watching TV, and my mother was in bed with a bad flu, when they pulled out number 14. "That's me, Mum." I heard a gasp from the bedroom. "But I shouldn't leave you. Maybe I can get an exemption, stay home and look after you."

"Don't be silly, son. You have to go. I'll be fine. I just pray they don't send you to that awful Asian place." She meant Vietnam, but because of the terrible stories and pictures coming across our small TV set, she couldn't bring herself to say the name.

Despite her wishes and her prayers, within a year, I found myself embroiled in a war nobody wanted. I was dropped into a horrible mess of testosterone and bloodshed. We fought the enemy physically and ourselves mentally. We drank ourselves silly whenever we could because we couldn't get over the horror and guilt. At first it was the guilt from taking a life when you remembered what you learned in Sunday School, *thou shall not kill*. But when it was kill or be killed, it became survivor guilt as we saw our colleagues being dragged back on stretchers screaming in pain, or if not so lucky, as dead as the litter they were carried out on.

And then in '72 the government changed and we were brought home. To a ticker-tape parade. To yells and screams of thankful hearts. To hats being thrown in the air. To congratulations for a job well done. To warm welcomes from the politicians and the keys to the city.

No.

No! Instead we returned to anti-war banners, to hatred, and to insults. We endured swearing and spitting, long queues and denials of welfare and, 'sorry we don't want you working here'. Worst of all, while I'd been away, my mother had died.

Six months later I was living in a pub in the middle of NSW, not talking to anyone, drinking so I could just make it through each day, crying every night. One morning in the second week, there was a documentary on the TV while I was eating lunch. A left-wing journalist was interviewing a movie star who'd travelled to North Vietnam. Before long the program was portraying our side as the criminals. Those who returned should be treated like convicts and my buddies who gave their lives were vilified. Certainly not heroes, at best they should be forgotten.

I tried to block it out but the pain was too much. I stood up and hurled my bottle of beer at the TV. It smashed, but the sound of the door slamming behind me was louder. I walked for hours trying to despatch the demons, then made a decision. I couldn't stay there any longer.

I went to the general store and bought a 1-man tent, swag, billy, utensils and a folding chair. In a gun shop I bought a .22 rifle and enough ammunition to last a month. I went up the stairs at the back of the hotel, grabbed my bag from the room and left a hundred bucks to pay for the damage.

The next three weeks I spent on my own in the forest by a fast though meandering stream. I set up my tent, readied a fire and went hunting rabbit. But in the third week, craving something other than rabbit, I shot a kangaroo. Unfortunately, the animal lashed out with a foot and opened up an old wound. After two days, I could hardly walk and felt ill. On the third day, worried about septicaemia, I left everything behind except my gun, and set out for the town. I didn't make it.

"Hello, where am I?" I asked when I saw a pretty nurse checking my chart.

"You're in the Narrabri Bush Nursing Hospital," she said as she took my blood pressure. "I'm Marlene. You were in a coma for two days. Although you did wake up screaming a couple of times. You're very lucky. Someone found you and brought you in. Another couple of days and you would have been history."

She smiled but I wasn't sure she was right. "Would've been best for everyone if I had," I groaned.

She was shocked. "No, don't say that." I tried to grin and nod and she asked, "We don't even know your name?"

"Brian."

The pretty girl wrote my name on her chart. "And where do you live, Brian?"

"Right here I think?" I tried to smile, but the pain wouldn't go away.

"No, I mean before this."

"Well, I used to live in Melbourne, but I sold up and came here. I haven't got an address. Narrabri Post Office, I guess."

"I'll use that then, bye."

She came back to check on me and gave me stronger pain meds. The next day I was sitting up a little when another woman walked in. She looked about my age. "Hello Brian, I'm Rebecca."

This woman wasn't as pretty as Marlene, but she was very attractive all the same. And she wasn't wearing a nurse's uniform. "Hello Rebecca, are you replacing Marlene?"

"No, Brian, I look after people in a different way." She was looking at the chart.

"Oh?"

"Your address is the post office. Obviously, you don't live there."

She gave me a beautiful smile.

"I guess the postmaster does, maybe I live with him?"

"Of course." I was sure she didn't believe it. "Where were you from before that? Do I detect a Victorian accent?" Marlene probably put something in the file. I nodded. I liked her, a lot.

"Can I call you Bec?"

"Luv, you can call me anything you like."

I started talking and she was a good listener. "In Melbourne I lived with mum. In St Kilda, just her and me, before — but she was sick and passed away."

"Sorry to hear that, Brian."

"After a bit I sold up. It was only a small flat." I didn't let on, there was a small debt on the property, and with my money from the army I paid it off and put it on the market. "I packed an overnight bag of everything I owned and hitchhiked out of there."

I didn't care where I was going, I just wanted to be on the road. Wanted to get as far away from the Army offices in St Kilda Road as I could manage. But I couldn't tell Bec that.

"So you hitchhiked all the way to Narrabri?" Bec was smiling again and I felt comfortable.

"More or less. I had lots of cars stop for me, male and female drivers."

"Brave women," she laughed.

"And a few trucks." I didn't tell her most of the time I was morose. Couldn't manage much of a conversation, and whenever I heard a car backfire, it set me off. "Took a while to get here. Made it to Shepparton, then Wagga and then a truck driver brought me all the way to Narrabri."

"That was a long trip."

"Yeah. The truck driver apparently tired of trying to make conversation and we listened to music the rest of the trip." Bec nodded and then became serious. I wondered what was coming.

But she put her hand on mine. "Brian, the police found your tent and belongings out in the bush. How long had you lived there?"

I tried to laugh but it came out wrong. "I didn't even last three weeks. Took a beating from a roo, nearly didn't make it."

"Yes I know that too. For a while it was touch and go." Bec patted my hand again before continuing. "Brian, you said something to Marlene that makes me think you're fighting demons inside."

I shook my head and started to say no, but the words wouldn't form in my mouth. Instead, my eyes started filling up.

Bec became serious once again, but her pager went off and she looked at the message and stood up. "Sorry Brian, I have to go. There's been a car accident on the highway. But I'll be back soon, I promise." She handed me a tissue for my eyes. "Don't go anywhere. Promise?"

I grinned. "I'm going to wait right here for you Bec."

"Thanks, Brian." She smiled her gorgeous smile and left the room.

I was sitting on a bench on the balcony the next afternoon when Bec joined me. "Marlene said I'd find you out here. I'm on my break, mind if I join you?"

I smiled and nodded and she sat down. My face must have given her the answer, but we didn't speak for a long time. I thought she'd fallen asleep and patted her hand. "You're a good sort, Bec." I suspected she wasn't on her break. I'd also gathered by then that she was a mental health nurse.

She smiled. "Brian, somewhere down deep inside, the real Brian is trying to get out. And I really want to meet that Brian."

I looked at her and felt my eyes water. I knew what she meant.

"But the chunks of your past life are smothering you."

"I know, I know," I shouted, tears now visible.

She held one hand while I wiped my tears with the other. After a while she put an arm on my shoulder. "I know your story Brian. Timmy was there too. I mean my brother Tim."

"From Nam?"

She told me the regiment, but I'd not come across them over there. "He was a great, happy guy before Vietnam. But it killed him."

"You don't mean the war do you?"

She shook her head, sat back down and started crying herself. "He went out into the paddock, Brian, took a rifle with him."

I started crying again and couldn't stop. "You could never understand, Bec."

She let me cry for a few minutes. "I do actually, Brian. I was there too."

It turned out she was in a field hospital that had been blown up.

"I was lucky to survive, most of our team didn't make it." She lifted her skirt and showed me an awful scar on her thigh.

"Did they ship you home?"

"No, patched me up and sent me to the next hospital."

"But, you seem so calm, so happy. You live at home?"

"I had to get out Brian. My folks would listen to the news and start saying Tim shouldn't have gone and I shouldn't have enlisted. Should have been conscientious objectors, the real heroes. I walked out one day and I haven't been back."

"Timmy didn't leave?"

Bec shook her head. "I wanted him to come with me."

"You were the sensible one."

Bec grabbed my hand again. "Brian, when you and I were over there, we knew who the enemy was. We could see them." She paused for a moment. "What did you do when they came at you?"

"I mowed them down. We threw everything we had at the enemy: rifles, machine guns, grenades."

"So who's the enemy now?"

I shouted. "Those guys out there, who didn't go!"

"Do you think?"

I didn't answer.

"So if you're right, can you mow them down?"

I shook my head. "Not a chance, no."

"No, you can't." She stopped talking for the longest time. When I looked at her, she wiped her eyes and continued. "But Brian *they're* not the enemy."

"What do you mean?"

She pointed to my head. "The enemy is in here." She shook my hand. "Brian, you have to come out of the shadows. Tim could never do that and it became too much."

When I finally stopped crying she said, "You can't live there." When I didn't speak she added, "It's like being beaten by a bully. Do you keep letting him knock you down?"

I managed to answer. "No, you stand up to him."

"Stand up to yourself, Brian."

After Bec left I stayed out there until dinner. After I'd eaten, I thought about what she'd said. Living in a tent in the bush wasn't facing up to the fight. I had to make a choice.

I don't remember making any decisions that night, but for once the dreams were in Narrabri and it was a beautiful sunny day. For the first time in three years, I woke up happy.

When Rebecca arrived at ten she stopped at the door. "Who are you, and what have you done with Brian?" I laughed with her and she sat on the bed. We shared stories about our childhood.

That afternoon I asked her where she lived. "I bought an old run-down house for two thousand dollars."

"Wow, that's cheap."

"Well it's not in Narrabri, it's ten miles up the road. The town is dying, people are moving to bigger towns or Sydney, and there are lots of nice houses to buy."

"No one wants an old run-down."

"Exactly."

"So what are you saying?"

"Do you still have money from the army?"

"Yes."

"There's one next door, I think it's even cheaper."

Two months later I moved into my new house. It was a rundown dump, but it was all mine. And I still had some savings in the bank.

About five o'clock one afternoon, I was in the back garden when I heard the latch move on the new gate between my property and the next. I'd been working all day. Despite the hot sun and pesky flies, I'd hardly stopped. It was great therapy. First I cleared undergrowth and debris from between the trees, and made a boundary of rocks. I used some of the broken tree branches to ready a campfire and secured my billy on top. Next I erected my tent, placed the swag inside and outside put the folding chair. As an afterthought, I went inside the house and returned with two rabbit skins. These I hung over a branch.

I was surveying my handiwork when Rebecca came through the gate and joined me. She picked up a sign lying on the ground. "Hi Brian, they've agreed to give you a casual position at the hospital."

"That's great Bec, thanks for doing that for me."

Bec didn't answer, she was looking at my work. "Looks like you've been hard at it." Grinning, I nodded and used my arm to wipe the sweat off my face. She had a frown on her face. "Is this going to be your special place?"

I picked up the mallet, took the sign from her and started hammering it into the ground in front of the tent. "No," I said. "Absolutely not. I've come out of there."

The sign read, '*The Shadows*'.

Winter High

J. Marahuyo

I step into a winter evening, watch
garra rufa fish swim through play smoke
from my 'O' shaped mouth and audible breath.
They bunch to suckle heat,
take turns to slap my round cheeks with frosty fins –
some even do it to my nose

I step into the Uber, say hi to the driver,
look over to see small brush strokes of a sleeve
on the fogged car window.
I stare out, pretend I'm a stranger.

I step into the house overspilling music and mood
lighting, make my way to the back to hug a friend
take a hit from the passing joint

e v e n i n g   f r i e n d   overspilling to a slo-mo
      He, a frosty suckle driver
                                        fogged back stare
hitting my 'O' sentences
   I step
         Hi eyes
                  Shape.   sleeve slap.
  take pretend step
                     to Stranger

I roll into a hug
step on leg sleeve
audible slap of Judgment, stroked with chill
I step
turn my fogged brain into some sentences

I'm a mood, slap, step, make face 'O'
shaping winter through my s l o - m o hugs
suckling on a man made of smoke
I swim, fish-step

I a fish swimming to alone
step, watch: heat leaving through nose
I s t a r e into forgetting
I. am. the. evening. watching.

I'm the car and the mood,
light leaving

Between the Speckled Lights

Gideon McDonald

This poem was awarded a *Highly Commended* in the poetry category of the Alice Sinclair Memorial Writing Competition.

brown Dirt, yellow Dirt, red Dirt I
look for the Dark spaces in the sky
Perhaps, that great flightless bird —
against eyes white, my white skin.

To focus on one pinprick, is to miss every other
performer: the canvas itself.

From somewhere humble; a dust-patch West of
Murchison,
the great expanse seen best from Shadow, it is as a
wise architect once wrote:

"If you want to know how much darkness there is
around you, you must sharpen your eyes, peering at
the faint lights in the distance."

For it is out here, in the Blackout, in the Dustbowl
that these
    // spaces between //   // the speckled lights //
exhibit so profoundly that most ancient pageantry. A celebration of the billowing massed curtains, of the ink and of the coal, the smouldering ash of the sky somewhere southwards.

So between this
brown Dirt, yellow Dirt, red Dirt I
look for the Dark spaces in the sky
eyes white —
this white skin,
                        Shapes, stories, memories.
Infantile, unknowing, I swallow, shimmer
for a moment,
            into this soothing sky …

The Short Story

Marie Heitz

The beginning of the beginning of twelve-year-old Billy Short's new life came when he saw the men's gymnastics final at the Beijing Olympics. Or specifically, it was when Billy saw the medal ceremony. He wasn't at the Olympics, of course.

He saw it on seven TV screens while standing in line at JB HiFi. Obviously they were on screens. Dudes like that didn't exist in real life; they belonged in Marvel movies, chucking hammers and belting up killer robots.

The guns on them! Not just dumb body-builder balloons, inflated by steroids, whose job was being looked at; the muscles on the gymnasts – so perfect they nearly made him moan – were the real business. With them, the men sprang and swung and whirled, iron wrists and scissoring legs; space and time and gravity were just toys they played with.

Their moves were stupid strong, impossible for real people. Especially on the rings: The Iron Cross: Billy laughed out loud. But the part that made him gasp was the medals presentation. There they were, three guys, two Chinese and a Romanian, shaking white-dusted hands, and here came the official, who was a giant. Then the camera panned to the support boxes filled with other athletes, and more giants.

No, there weren't any giants. All the athletes – the artist gods – were *short.* Barely taller than him. The bubble of possibility expanded in his chest till it literally stopped him breathing.

"So? You're going to buy something, or just here to watch the TV?" The shaved head behind the counter had a tiger tatt crawling up out of his shirt onto his jaw, which seemed to claw his ear as he spoke.

Billy looked down at the Nintendo console he'd been saving for. Six months it had taken him. It was a part of his old life now. Up to five minutes ago it had been the best part. "No," he said. "Changed my mind."

By the time his uncle Ferdy got home, Billy had eaten his dinner, finished his homework, researched gymnastic training and created a Solution. Ferdy didn't do problems. He was too busy. Billy knew he could usually have what he wanted if it was a Solution.

Ferdy was at his laptop eating rewarmed sausages with his fingers and typing with the other hand. He pushed his glasses back with the heel of his hand.

"So, Saturdays, you get to the lessons on your bike, you won't need equipment except maybe some shoes and you can pay for everything yourself."

"Yep. I didn't buy the Wii console."

Ferdy looked mildly surprised. "Ok, then. Mo doing it with you?"

"No." Mo was going to be bummed. It couldn't be helped. Besides, Mo had soccer.

"Ok." Ferdy licked a finger and frowned at his screen. "We good then?"

"You have to sign a form saying I could get injured but we don't blame them."

Billy shoved the form he'd printed and a pen next to Ferdy's plate. His uncle did read it before he signed.

"Thanks." As predicted, no opposition but not much interest either. His uncle provided the vital stuff: a safe home, food, clothes, reliability, which was a million times better than his mum had. For interest in himself, as well as the official reason which was maths tutoring, Billy had Angela. Except one day Angela would graduate and become a doctor and leave. Billy wished Ferdy would marry Angela, so they could keep her, but he was far too old.

And of course, because Ferdy was Billy's mother's brother, he was too short.

The man his mother had claimed was his father had denied it all the way up to the DNA test. Then he still denied it on the basis that if he'd wanted to be a father, he wouldn't have worn a condom. He explained Billy as a sperm which was so small, the little bastard could swim through the condom, a theory which covered all the known facts.

Angela wasn't due till tomorrow and his first gymnastics session wasn't till the day after that, which was Saturday.

Billy spent the evening looking up beginner gymnastic exercises, which were supposed to teach him Strength, Agility and Flexibility. The beginner classes already used the Men's equipment: Vault, Pommel, Parallel Bars, High Bars and the ultimate, Rings. He clenched his fists. Yesss! And Floor, but that didn't count.

Baby stuff.

Though if he was going to practice any of these routines at home — which he was, he'd practice every day, in the time he'd played video games before — the floor was all he had. His floor could become Floor. He could start right now!

"Hi Ange! You're early."

Angela was letting herself in the front door. She wore calf length tights, Blundstones and an ancient black denim jacket and had lots of copper coloured frizzy hair and freckles. The freckles were standing out just now and her eyes were doing that laser beam thing that always made Billy think he'd hate to see her really mad.

"Let me guess. The Mullets started already?" he asked.

She snorted. "You got it." Angela shared a house with three members of the Mullet Skulls, a death metal band. They called themselves the Skulls — Angela and Billy didn't — and they practised in the garage, which they'd sound-proofed, more or less. Fortunately, Mr Hendricks, their garage side neighbour, used to work in a foundry, was deaf and said the sound he could hear made him nostalgic. Angela wasn't deaf, so she'd made an arrangement with Ferdy that on practice nights, she'd study at their place.

Billy and Angela's routine, which Billy would have approved even if it wasn't Angela who proposed it, was they'd sit in the kitchen, Angela would drink horrible Yaupon tea and Billy apple juice, and they'd chat for ten minutes then they'd move to Billy's room and do strictly nothing but maths for an hour. Then they'd move back to the kitchen and chat what still needed to be chatted.

Angela had soon found out that Billy wasn't actually bad at maths. He was bad at coping in maths class, only nominally controlled by Mr Fairly, who was balding in his twenties, with eyes that floated like pale jellyfish in the thick portholes of his glasses, while eczema and acne fought over the remaining territory of his face. He was totally outmatched by Bode Lewis and Jayden Pike, the class bullies.

Billy found their torment of the teacher harder to deal with than the spitballs, having his tablet constantly knocked to the floor, or his chair replaced with a Grade 1 sized one. Disorder made Billy anxious. Chaos made him panic. Numbers calmed him. They were clearcut and dependable and discovering the order in the patterns they made was an infinitely repeatable pleasure. And he got to do it with Angela.

Billy was going to save his news till after the maths because he was good at saving things and it was serious news. But only ten minutes into the hour, Angela drummed her nails on the desk. "Okay, 313% of people hate statistics, but that's not your problem today. What gives?"

Billy looked at his phone. "But our rule ..."

"Our rules, ours to bend. We can make up the time later. Just now, we're wasting it." She drew both forefingers like handguns and took aim on the poster near the window. "My guess is it's to do with Captain Falcon's rip."

Angela was good at noticing things, which Billy thought would make her a good doctor. Captain Falcon indeed had a tear right across the ridiculous muscle of his blue thigh. Billy had mended it with sticky tape, but the Cap was going to be permanently slower than Sonic the Hedgehog, that's if he ever got to run again, which Billy wasn't sure about.

"I can show you." Billy put his back to the door to give himself room, then somersaulted across the floor, with his Converses slapping against the opposite wall, awkwardly on either side of the Cap. "That's a somersault," said Billy. He went back to the door. This time, he bent his knees, put his hands to the floor and flexed his head to his chest, went over much faster in a compact ball, pushing back to a stand a metre from the Captain, who looked sternly pleased. "And that's a forward roll," Billy said. "I didn't put weight on my head or my neck and I held my knees in until the end."

Angela clapped. "I see why the Captain preferred the forward roll. But wait, there's more?" she said.

"This is something I," Billy jabbed his chest — narrow, bony, but that would change, "could be good at. Kohei Uchimura, King Kohei, was five foot three and he won three all-round Olympic gold medals. So was Yang Wei. Arthur Zanetti, he's Brazilian, the boss of the rings, he's more jacked than anyone, he's five foot one!" Billy's voice was almost squeaking. He sounded like a mouse. He lowered it, sat down but jumped up again. "I'm kind of old to get started at twelve, but Kurt Thomas was fifteen, and men champions are older than women."

Angela fisted the air. "Awesome! I'm sure if you put your mind to it, you're going to be very very good. Should we declare a maths holiday today and you can show me some more stuff?"

"No." Billy sat down again. "Even Olympic gymnasts don't make money, so I still need to finish school."

"Are you sure you're twelve?" Angela grinned. "Okay, onward, then! Look out, standard deviations, here we come!"

That night, just before Billy turned out his light, Captain Falcon exchanged a sombre look with his F-Zero nemesis, the Black Shadow, on the wall opposite. They knew their time was done.

It was a week before Billy saw Angela again. She was even earlier this time. The Skulls had their first actual gig coming. Their playing needed to match the standard of their really excellent snarling and brooding.

They were practicing frantically every moment they got. So it being only 4pm, it was no surprise Billy wasn't in the hall to greet her. She walked into the kitchen and stopped. "Shit, Billy! What happened?"

He'd been bending over the kitchen sink and turned to face her. At first she thought he'd been vomiting blood. His face was streaked and blotched bright red, his mouth a grotesque facsimile of a clown's smile, smeared down his chin onto his neck.

"I'm ok," he said, though he plainly wasn't. Angela's heart turned over at the despair in his eyes. "It's lipstick." He scrubbed at it with the dishcloth in his hand. His forearm was criss-crossed with scratches. "How do you get it off?"

"Uh –" No makeup remover. "Olive oil would work."

There was a bottle on the bench behind him. She stepped closer and reached for it. Billy had two fingernail sized glittery pink and gold patches on his shirt. And more in his hair. Stickers. Of little blonde girls in tutus.

"Billy …"

His jaw was trembling. "It was Bode and Jayden. Bode's house is three up from the gymnastics gym. He saw me come out of class, with all the girls. They've been sticking these things on all my stuff all week. And today they were waiting for me." He looked her in the face, rigid with misery. "I can't go again. They'll never stop." His eyes brimmed over.

And so passed the beginning of the beginning of Billy's new life.

But he'd started now, and wherever he went, he wasn't going back. He hadn't realised it yet, but Angela had.

She didn't try to hug him or say it was ok to cry. She ignored his tears, so he could too.

She sat down at the table and said, "Did I ever tell you I was hell on a skateboard? I've still got my first deck. It's your size."

Antidote

Kathryn Fry

Sun in a halo of cloud, sky a riffraff of high
uncertain shapes, some breaking away
troubling the land across the lake, above

the stark glint on windows near the water.
Thornbills flit by an old grey gum and no wonder
as last night's rain summoned a soak slipping

to a stream of bubbles over the path; how lucky
you think, to be here. Whipbirds, honeyeaters
and ravens drum up a tinpot band but the show

flares with the sulphur-crested cockatoos
before the next sudden shower. Wind thrums
with cool scents and moisture; people you pass

seem open and warm; you feel your shortcomings
stowed aside. Three butterflies lift up their wings.
And before you hear today's news of harrowing

suffering and black hope, of conflict and stormy
fraud, those darkest stains, you stand stilled
as light turns wet leaves into ripples of shimmer.

SECTION 5

BEATING BACK THE BLOWS ...

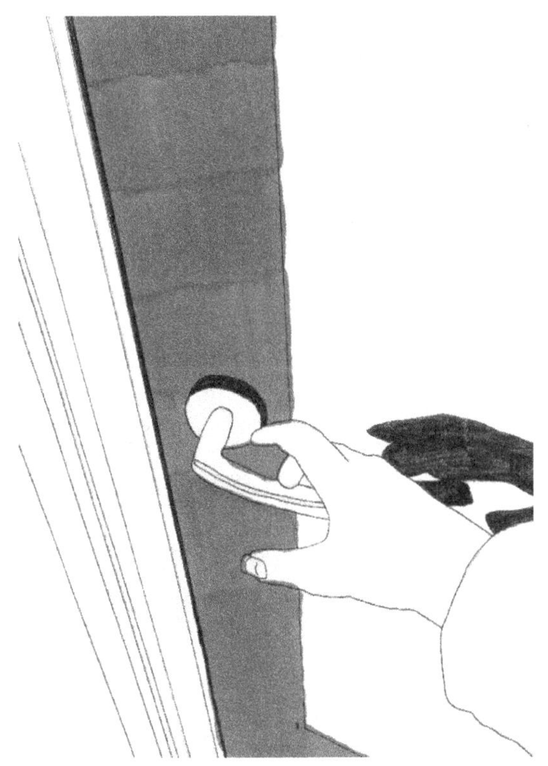

Eleven Steps

Rees Campbell

Waking
He rolls over, into the hollow
and hugs his love
A couple of minutes of dreamy
Before the alarm drills a hole into his brain
He slaps it off, and staggers to the bathroom
for a piss …
feeling the bedwarm leave his body
with the steady stream

Washes the gritty residue
of last night's late shift
from his eyes
Dresses while the coffee gurgles
Drinks the brew as black and bitter as his thoughts

Leaving,
he blows his sleepy love a kiss
Unfelt, unheard and unacknowledged
Uses half his outside time
in eleven steps to the car

Everything shaded slatey grey
in the winter city dawn
Only a black cat watches from the shadows
slit eyes gleaming
Drives on empty streets to work
and feels the churning anticipation start

Inside
the harsh bright lights illuminate
a brave new world
and he starts to camouflage
until he becomes
"a health worker"
clad in blue plastic smock
blue face mask
blue gloves
visor
the only thing rendering him unique
is the stuck-on name tag

Exhausted
8 hours later
He strips the layers
of protection
of plastic waste
from sweaty skin

And heads for home
in the dank early night
of winter city dusk
Eleven steps to the front door
of a cold dark empty house

No wonder he drinks

R & R

Sinead Reilly

1

I'm not sure what time it is. Late. I can tell because I can't hear any cars passing by. I usually can. Shadows of the tree outside my window are spilling across my ceiling. I can hear nothing save for the wind.

I concentrate on trying to lie perfectly still in the dark. I can't remember it ever being this dark.

I am starting to feel as though I am floating in a tank when I register the first yelp. An animal. I think it's a cat, but upon hearing it again, it's clearly a dog. Must be my neighbour's dog — the young guy a bit further up. Don't know his name. The place that separates our houses has been vacant for a time. A nice young couple lived there long enough to realise they probably needed better. That was about a year ago, and the 'For Sale' sign is still up. Sunburnt now, peeling round the edges, and the photos are all faded too.

I try to listen more closely. The shadows continue to gambol about on the ceiling. If I don't blink, they get bigger and bigger.

After a few minutes I hear another whine. It's not really a whine, but I don't know how else to describe it. I haven't heard anything like it. I don't want to believe that it's a dog making that sound. A flurry of barks every so often means I can't fool myself much longer. The neighbours on the other side don't have any pets. Just the one guy there alone for as long as I've been here and probably twenty years more. I shouldn't be able to hear the dog from here.

Only minutes have passed before I hear it again. And again. The furiously dancing patterns, faster and faster, falling into and over each other — extricating contorting unfolding — transfix my sight in the still dark. Again. I shut my eyes.

I try to think of the last time I saw the dog. Can't think of her name, or how she looked. I know she's a retriever, white gold one. I like those ones. The yellow ones are alright. I can't think of whether I ever asked her name or how old she is or when the neighbour brought her home or anything much at all, not even what he looks like. Around my height maybe. Closing my eyes hasn't done much good at all. It's still going.

2

When I wake, the birds outside my window are calling to each other. They sound listless this morning. Feeble. They're probably not because birds can't really be listless or feeble unless they're sick or dying but maybe they can be.

An ex-girlfriend of mine kept a parrot that always looked sort of miserable. Pulled out a bunch of its feathers once. She said it was stressed. I ended up letting it out the window and it probably didn't last much longer after that.

The sky is strewn with watery ink and some thin clouds, and acid from my stomach coats the back of my throat.

Fast-forward three blank months and I can remember little else but the sound of the dog getting kicked — which now seems optimistic — half to death every Friday night.

I don't know why it only happens on Fridays. I don't think there is a reason. The guy could just clock off work and go have some beers like everyone else, but that doesn't seem to be on his agenda.

Strewn between the melting months have been increasingly desperate attempts to get a hold of someone at the police station that won't promise a call back and then not call back.

I get through.

I don't want to fixate on what the woman sounded like, or even what she said when I asked why they haven't been answering the phone. I don't even think I asked. Not important. I was just happy that someone finally picked up.

The voice — Carolina, I wrote it down — informed me that two officers will visit my neighbour's house on Thursday. Today is Sunday.

I told her that the dog gets beat up on Fridays — a visit on Thursday might be too late. What if he's not home, what if he's at work or the supermarket or takes his car to the mechanic, he has a job, he works, it's a nine to five job and that's all I know, I haven't spoken to the guy much but he does work and he goes out after work too, he really isn't home that much but I also don't know because I don't keep tabs on what the guy does at every waking moment but maybe I should if they can't arrange to visit after five or earlier in the week.

Carolina asks me to please calm down. She's chewing gum. I want to hang up but there's a good chance that the dog would be in the ground by the time I manage to get through again.

I say thank you, make sure the officers do visit, thank you and goodbye.

Pieces of broken glass swim innocently in water on my kitchen floor. It's spattered all over the bit of paper I'd written my neighbour's address on. I watch as the letters bleed into each other slowly. It's sodden. I don't remember smashing the glass.

Trying not to think about the retriever, I pick up the slivers of glass and clean the water up. Snowy white fur matted with dark blood. My hands are shaking a little. Big soft ears.

3

Today is Thursday, and I've taken the day off work. Predictably, my neighbour is gone already. I need a day off anyway. I pace around my house and yard, caged, waiting for the officers to turn up as per Carolina's bidding.

I wait all day.

At around three, a flock of schoolgirls glides down the street. Snatches of their laughter float in through my windows.

They don't show up.

4

I wake in the early hours of Friday morning to the shrieks of the dog. My neighbour has tweaked his schedule slightly. Rest and recuperation. I lie in bed awhile with some music turned up full volume, trying not to picture violent things happening to him.

Getting into my car, I drive through the night until the hard dark sky is tempered a little by the dawn. Settling on radio voices talking about nothing much in particular, I turn the volume up to maximum and put all the windows down. The cool wind whips through the car and stays with me and I can't hear the voices talking at me at all.

Eventually I pull over by someone's field. The house is all dark and far away.

Ducking through the barbed wire fence, I lie down in the long grass. I don't know why people bother with barbed wire. The ground has been softened by rain and I'm trespassing, I have to get back in time for work but the sunrise is coming up all embarrassed pink and lunchbox yellow and the retriever's ears and snowy bloody fur …

5

Friday night is, unusually, something of a respite. Wonder what's up with him.

The following morning, I wait for my neighbour to go to work. He's listening to some pop rubbish as he drives away. I guess the wailing voices help drown out his conscience.

Tucking some old blankets under my arm, I turn down the narrow pathway leading to his backyard from the street. I didn't know how many I'd need so I brought them all. The front gate is abnormally small, so I push it open with my foot. I let myself into the backyard via the cracked path beside the house.

It takes me a few minutes to find her. She's in the shed and can't walk on her own. I think some of her bones must be broken. Gingerly, I wrap her up in the blankets and she whines with pain when I pick her up off the stained concrete. She's feather light, much too light. I'm sorry, I'm sorry, I'm sorry. Liquid brown eyes look up at me as I carry her down the street with soft steps. The pavement feels warm under my feet, radiating through my shoes and into my legs.

The vet asks a lot of pointed questions. I don't blame him.

Later, at home, I carefully wash her snowy fur. I'm lathered up to my elbows in red soapy foam. I gently towel her dry, smiling beatifically all the while.

After a couple of days go by, my neighbour knocks on the door. One-two-three.

I briefly consider ignoring it before deciding otherwise. I don't want him to get any ideas.

He's smiling one of those smiles where you can see all the teeth, and his hair is matted to his forehead a bit. I instantly want to close the door.

He tells me where he lives – as if I didn't know – and asks whether I've seen his dog. I think a moment before shaking my head and telling him I'll keep an eye out.

Yeah, he says. Please do. He hasn't blinked this whole time.

I close the door.

Epiphany

Agi Dobson

She didn't kill herself when things went wrong *
but walked out in the roaring wind
held her face up to the sky
inviting thunder
inviting rain
she stood for an hour
maybe more –
none came.

The wind freed her hair from its tight chignon
whipping it loose around her face
stopping her tears like any slap.
She turned back.
Shedding bracelets and rings
her dress from Vuitton
shoes from Prada
a leafless tree – thus
happier, naked.

She stands. Tranquil, free of artifice
in a humble black dress
hair tumbling down
a black cascade
peeling, paring away
the layers of untrue –
wholesome as an apple
the truth is always plain.

She needs no adornment – but for
a bow in her hair for hope
red lips painted for passion.
A brown fowl is her guide, to
show the simple path
– her egg a gift
latent as a promise
to be discovered
when she takes that last step, to
emerge from the final shadow.

This poem was inspired by an oil painting, *Dressed in Cohen,* by John Mutsaers.

* First line from Leonard Cohen's, *The Only Poem:* "I didn't kill myself /when things went wrong".

Reckoning

Kim Michelle Ross

Another afternoon spent alone behind locked doors and barred windows, but she enjoyed these stolen moments of sweet serenity, for it'd fade in an instant when he came home. Melodic poundings drifted from the outside world. From somewhere in the dark recesses of her memory she knew it was a song called *Gangsta's Paradise*.

She'd heard it a long time ago, back in another lifetime when she knew how it felt to be alive.

A picture of an angry black man laden in heavy gold chains filled her mind, but something deeper had woken the past.

Bad thoughts returned.

Desperately she tried burying the horrors of that summer's day; it'd been a day much like today. Fists scrunched into tight balls.

She glared at the walls that imprisoned her. She wished the musical vibrations would make them collapse.

This house was her entire world, beyond that was out-of-bounds. In here she wallowed in an emptiness that refused to let her feel, at least nothing got through except the hurt never left.

"Someday, I hope I can forget," she whispered.

A car horn blared. She jumped. The rap music coming from next-door stopped.

There was a long silence, minutes later a door slammed, then a young man yelled, "Hurry up babe."

Curiously she peered through the barred windows, her eyes smarting from the day's brightness. Pangs of envy surfaced. She was envious of Evie, the girl who lived next-door. Then she wondered about Evie's little brother, the memory of the child was a sad reminder, and she relived the loss all over again.

It was painful watching Evie sliding into her boyfriend's car and seeing her kiss him.

Shock hit her hard — she hadn't realised so many years had passed; Evie looked about sixteen or eighteen, she was a little girl of six the last time she saw her.

"I don't want to live like this anymore. I want to feel again …"

The sound of her rarely used voice sounded strange and distant, as if it didn't really belong to her. Then again, she usually only managed to make muffled noises through the gag when she tried to scream. She was grateful he stopped tying her to the bed, and removed the chain that'd once seemed fused to her ankle.

Love so soft and giving was getting difficult to remember. Her mind clouded with the nightmarish shades of fear. Inside, she felt dead. She slapped her face. Stinging numbness tingled her cheek and reddened her palm.

"Pain, that's all I know." Salty tears spilt over her quivering lips.

Saltiness; a reminder of a beautiful moment, and then it merged with her mother's awful warnings as she lay on the kitchen floor, as rivers of red flowed from deep gashes in both of her arms. Her bloody fingers grasped her hands as her mother gasped, "Run," through bloodied lips before her final words. "Hide, keep your bedroom door locked …"

She hadn't run because it was too late. He stood in the doorway. Luckily, he hadn't seen her; she hid under the sink. The commotion didn't last and life continued and yet it seemed normal. But over the years since her mother's death, her father changed. Everything changed. She kept telling herself adolescent girls simply don't disappear. Yet, every night she'd wake to the sound of a turning key in the lock of her bedroom door, followed by urgent rattles of the doorknob. She was glad Davey put a bolt on the inside of it.

Dashing to the sideboard, she dug out the precious photograph from its special hiding place, a secret compartment at the back of the drawer; she was grateful he never knew it existed. It had to stay hidden. If he knew she'd kept it he'd probably kill her. Then again, death would be better than merely existing. Her fingertips gently brushed dusty layers from the only image of the only love she'd known.

As she stared at it, she was lost within the tarnished frame. Her heart swelled. She spoke his name, "Davey," and caressed the stilled image that'd captured his angelic features. His innocent smirk beamed, his startling blue eyes shone, and he had a cheeky smile that held wisdom beyond his years. His sun-bleached hair dangled into his eyes. She recalled tussling those unruly sea-salt-encrusted curls.

They'd been silly teens at the beach when this picture was taken, on a day much like today. They'd made plans, she was going to run away and live with her maternal grandparents, and Davey was going to visit, and she'd be safe —

The front door banged.

She put the picture away; sweet memories of startling blue were replaced by nefarious miscreant slits.

Heavy footfalls bounded down the hall. Something crashed. Profanities flowed. Dreaded fear choked the remnants of the hope that'd sprung from within her darkened depths, and then with a sickening twist, hope was gone.

Her mother's dying warnings rebounded inside her mind. She wanted to run, but it was too late, she'd never get away in time.

The door flung wide. He sauntered in. "Humph. Place's a bloody mess!"

"I'm sorry, I waited. You promised to take me …" Her words trailed.

"What? So, *it* can speak when *it* wants to — you're not going anywhere *ever*, you have to make me dinner, clean this fecking house, and then service me."

"But you said you'd take me to see Davey if I asked nicely —"

"*Stupid cow* — what makes you think I'll ever let you go anywhere. Ya can't see the dead. Yeah, and I did it 'cos he took something that belonged to *me*. You're mine. He'll never touch you again."

The cold fierceness in his laugh bit hard. Now she knew there really was a hardened hole where her heart used to be. It surprised her that even that empty space was capable of shattering like a piece of fragile crystal.

His cruel promise had been a pipedream. The torture gave him pleasure. Another clear reminder to her battered body: *you can't fight the things that hunt you.*

"Seeing you've done nothing all day — get on your knees." He unzipped his fly, and his large grubby hands grabbed her shoulders, forcing her head towards his fleshy groin. His sour breath sailed above her. His fat, sweaty body revolted her anew. The depths of her core sparked, and she heard a tiny voice inside her head. *This time you must run, take back the power, time for the hunted to become the hunter…*

She shoved his burly frame away.

"*No,*" she shrieked. "No-no-no — *you're never touching me again.*"

She ran to the kitchen. Frightened eyes stayed focused on the doorway as her desperate hands blindly rummaged through the utensil draw. Then her fingers curled around a hard plastic handle; she felt its metal length, sleek and cool. She drew it out studying its multi-razor toothed edge from its steely sheath to its sharp pointed tip. It caught the glint of the afternoon sunshine streaming through the bars on the kitchen windows.

His shadowy figure filled the doorway.

"Girly," he calmly said. He was staring. He seemed stunned and pale, yet he continued to stalk his way towards her, unable to hide his predatory nature.

"Come on, put it down. Don't be playing with knives — don't point it at me. Be a good girl and just, put it down ... I promise, I'll take you to see him ... tomorrow, or the next day, maybe this weekend. But ya gotta think about what people will say if you're seen. Cops blame you for killing your mother, and as for that kid …"

She smirked. His voice was quivering, it sounded weak. Could he be pleading with her? Then she wondered if that's the way she sounded. He always ignored her pleas whenever she screamed *no* and *don't*. He'd just laughed, gagged her, then depravedly used her any way he wanted.

"No," was all she said.

She lunged, aiming for his grotesquely rotund gut. It was swift. It was like watching the precision knife point in slow motion. Instead of finding his stomach, it plunged deep and hard within his gullet; its handle prevented it from going completely through his throat.

He gasped.

"Bastard," she shrieked. "This is for you and all of your paedophile mates, and for the things you did to me. And for the things you did to those other girls you hid in the basement. Mum killed herself because of *you* — I've done nothing wrong — you're a sick twisted creature!"

She felt pleasure as she drew out the blade, and then stuck it back in, and she kept going. Jagged metal sawed and gnawed his insides like a hungry wildcat devouring a hapless wildebeest, gnashing as it plundered its prey, till at last, he stopped twitching.

Calmly, she dropped the knife and removed her blood-soaked clothes, and left them in a pile beside his corpse. She moved as if she were in a dream and showered away her hate-fuelled bloodletting. Then she wished the warming spray could have easily cleanse the years of his rapaciousness that began after a day at the beach.

A blurred image swam before her eyes. She recalled their young bodies, sultry and tanned, enjoying their first sensual time together, then he caught Davey in her bed; she'd forgotten to lock the door. Immediately the darkness descended. Ribbons of red mingled with heady metallic scents that sprayed across her walls, that's all she remembered. Davey disappeared and she never saw him again.

Weeks later she heard they found Davey's body, and by then she was dead inside, except for the little life growing inside her. She had no idea if it was Davey's, or his.

The police found someone to blame for Davey's murder, a homeless sod. There wasn't a scrap of evidence connecting her father to a notorious paedophile ring that was kidnapping adolescent girls between the ages of twelve and seventeen. Why would the authorities suspect an everyday Dad who'd reported his daughter missing on the same day Davey disappeared. She was another statistic on an ever-increasing list of local missing daughters. Though most of them were found – raped and dead by strangulation.

They didn't even bother connecting her disappearance with the murder of a teenage boy. The police had no reason to search their cellar, but if they had, they'd have uncovered more bodies of missing girls aged from twelve to seventeen.

Her belly grew so big, the sight of it disgusted him. When the pains came, she was frightened, she wanted to save her child, but it was hopeless, she couldn't save herself. What if he replaced her with his granddaughter, or would his sadistic nature compel him to groom a grandson into becoming a monster? And she often wondered what would happen when he finally outgrew her?

She glimpsed the baby when it was born, and knew it was Davey's – it made her happy knowing part of him still survived. But her joy was short-lived, he took the baby away, and she never knew if it was a boy or a girl.

A few days later she heard a baby's cries coming from next door. Through her bedroom window she spotted six-year-old Evie playing on the front porch and a newborn in a bassinette; a baby boy with golden hair, and the spitting image of Davey. She overheard Evie telling the postman that her new little brother was adopted.

Finally, she was clean, though the house resembled a slaughterhouse. She was glad he was gone, yet she still wasn't completely free. With little effort she constructed two detailed letters.

She left one on the sideboard addressed to the police, the other was for the next-door neighbours. Then she took all the cash from his blood-sodden wallet. Packed a tote bag. Called a cab. Locked the house, and then she slipped her letter into Evie's mailbox.

It felt good to be outside. She basked in the dusky atmosphere as she waited for her ride. The air was fragrantly fresh and filled with the chirps of cicadas.

"Davey," she cooed, as she felt Davey's picture inside the bag, "I'm coming to find you."

The taxi arrived, she jumped in, and slid across the backseat.

"Where to love?" the cabbie asked.

"Sandgate Cemetery." The only address she knew to begin searching.

She felt lost wandering through what seemed to be endless rows of graves, till just before dawn, she came upon his headstone.

Sitting down beside it she delved into her bag, drew out a box of pills, a bottle of vodka and Davey's photo; she gazed lovingly at his youthful features. She swallowed a pill, then washed it down with a swig of vodka, and repeated the sequence till the pills were gone, and the booze was empty.

"Davey," she whispered. A tear rolled down her cheek and splashed onto the picture. She kissed the glass, it tasted of salt. She smiled. It was as if she'd been transported to the beach on a warm summer's day. She sensed Davey's presence, he was near, and the world became hazy. She saw him standing inside a bright light – though he was still far away. Somehow, she knew he'd been waiting for her.

"Not much longer, Davey, I'll see you soon ... we'll run away as we planned, and be together forever."

She laid her head upon the grave, closed her eyes, feeling the pills taking effect. "Now," she mumbled, "I'm truly free ..."

Words From Beyond

Christine Johnson

I grew up with my Auntie Madge. We lived far from any big centre, in an old place just up the road from susso town. The shanties had spread a fair way by then. People called times hard. Depression. That was the name bandied about.

Auntie Madge did clearance sales, drove miles, travelling pot-holed tracks to outlying homesteads, selling stuff on that she brought back in the old van. Junk it was, but that trading business knocked her out a living. It was her hard yakka that stopped us being skint and kept food on our table. Other than that, she kept herself to herself. Brought me up to do the same.

Locals were shy of her, some backing off when they saw her coming. There were folks reckoned Auntie Madge was a witch. That included Charlie Mortenson.

"Your bloody aunt! She cursed my Ma, spooked Pa and made him bolt," he said, bailing me up in the schoolyard one day.

Charlie was bigger than other kids. Whatever he said, they agreed, for fear he'd pick on them.

Like most of my age, I'd worked out quick it was best to watch your back. Look out for some kid ready to twist your arm or punch you, push you over and sneer as you scrambled away. Kids like that never got bored with being mean. They only crowed louder to their mates about how often and in how many ways they'd put you down, before singling out their next target and moving on.

Charlie Mortenson. He was a boy like that.

But this time when Charlie swore again, calling Auntie Madge a worse than usual awful name, I lunged. I saw red and, like something wild, flew at him. Later, Auntie Madge laid a damp rag over my blackening eye.

"*Did* you bite him?" she asked. "Teacher reckons you almost took off his ear."

No point lying. She sniffed out a furphy quicker than anyone.

"Quicker than a fart on a church pew," as Charlie Mortenson jeered at me after our fight. He said she'd bail me up for the blue.

"Yes, Auntie."

She chuckled. "Best rinse your mouth in that case. Lad like that — dog bites him, it'll be the dog catches rabies."

I steered clear of Charlie after that, like Auntie Madge told me. Better to turn tail and run, live to fight another day.

"That Mortenson lot are bad," she said. "Mark my words. Stick to their right side, if you can find it. That, or steer clear altogether."

It was true. Give Charlie a hard time, and Charlie's older brother Wayne Mortenson and his mob were likely to show up. Wayne in his dilapidated tilted Homburg, the others with their cloth caps, all with clenched fists and ugly looks on their faces, they'd arrive. Threaten to thrash you, or worse.

Locals for miles around muttered about the things those bullies got up to. Like how they'd ripped off old Widow Gilbert's truck one time, setting it on fire. Although Wayne's Ma swore blind to the local cop her sons, Wayne and Charlie both, were home.

Who would have thought that six months after Charlie Mortenson landed a black eye on me, he'd be in the ground? A mouthful of dirt filling his mouth where curse words used to be. Nine years old, a little older than me, he'd gone.

At the funeral I sat silent. Watched the locals' eyes fix, suspicious, on the coffin as if it'd burst open; show them Charlie had sucked them in as usual with another of his mean pranks. I listened, stunned, to Father O'Hara describing Charlie as 'our dear departed boy,' even calling him 'an angel'.

"Nice service, Father," Auntie Madge said as we left the church.

The priest nodded. They only put up with each other. Auntie Madge reckoned he had tickets on himself. He thought her rough as bags; suspected his funerals were part of her trading business, showing where the next deceased estates would crop up.

Auntie Madge tucked her thin cardigan round her. We wended our way through the gravestones towards the parked van. I knew the stones well. From an early age Auntie Madge often brought me here.

"Best way to get to know your neighbours," she'd say. "Meet them at their quietest."

My little fingers traced these lolling monuments, learning my numbers and alphabet. Today, they gave me the shivers.

I sat in the van as it bounced along the track, whipping up a cloud of twirling dust. The vehicle rattled over the corrugations, jarring my bones. Tense, I clung to the edge of the battered seat. When we reached our back door, Charlie Mortenson was still on my mind.

"Auntie, will Charlie go to heaven?"

"That's between him and the Lord."

"But I mean, *Charlie Mortenson*. He ..."

Even if I'd found the words to spill what I needed to share, Auntie Madge silenced me with a frown.

"Never speak ill of the dead," she warned.

Inside, I set a pan of water to boil while Auntie Madge cleared a space, sat and opened the newspaper. She smoothed it out before taking up a stub of a pencil to circle obituaries.

I was used to the house being a carnival and curse of treasures and trash. On her rounds, Auntie Madge turned up lots of stuff. She haggled well and, glad to send her on her way, few people gave her a knockback.

Some things she gave special attention to. Letters dead people couldn't throw away she found stuffed into the backs of old couches. Or maybe a baby blanket and a tiny lock of hair secreted in a trunk at a deceased spinster's house.

As I watched her one day, sifting through the latest bric-à-brac she'd got hold of, she stopped.

"Ever wonder why they call me a witch?"

"They don't."

She waved her hand. "Save your breath."

I blushed.

"It's because they come, see, wanting to speak to their dead," she explained. "Words from beyond make grieving easier. It's extra cash on the side. Hurts no one and settles some."

After that, I spied on Auntie Madge at work.

One old lady was a regular. She came to chat to her dead handyman husband, about things like her removing a cupboard he'd built, to make way for a newfangled refrigerator. Auntie Madge would nod, close her eyes, lift her chin and tilt her head as if listening.

"He had a rough spin with that cupboard," she said. "Hit his thumb with the hammer twice, making it. If he was here, he'd pull the blasted thing out himself."

The old lady left, all smiles. Auntie Madge counted notes.

"That's the gas bill," she said, folding money into an old tea tin.

"Why do you charge?"

"People only value what's paid for."

When the water boiled the afternoon of Charlie Mortenson's funeral, I sat with Auntie Madge to drink our tea. My mind was still turning over words, battling with the shadows, trying to think of a way to tell what I knew. There came a knock at the front door. Auntie Madge went to answer it. From the kitchen, I listened.

The upset voice was familiar. I froze. It was the Widow Gilbert.

Everything came flooding back.

Charlie Mortenson, after he'd stopped picking on me, looked around and chose his next target. He wanted to impress his brother Wayne's friends, get a guernsey amongst them. His favourite trick became showing how grown up he was by skiting about what he got away with at the Gilbert's place.

Frank Gilbert, the Widow's boy, was a mean choice. A grown man, near thirty-years old I reckon, but slow — how slow depended on who you listened to.

The woman running the local store said Frank couldn't write his name, let alone read a sentence. The garage bloke said Frank fixed an engine good as him, but couldn't tell the time. Some reckoned Frank hit his head when he was six and it knocked everything he'd yet to learn out of his skull.

My heart thumped as Auntie Madge showed the Widow into our back room, empty except for a table and chairs. I crept into the store cupboard and put my eye to a crack. This was the way I always spied upon Auntie Madge dealing with her clients.

"You've got to help my lad. He's all I got," Widow Gilbert said. "What they're claiming ain't right. He wouldn't harm a flea."

"Wait up Mrs Gilbert, what can I do? Your Frank isn't dead," my aunt said.

"But he's arrested, thrown in a cell and already there's talk of hanging," the Widow said. "No. You got to get the truth, out of that dead one, Charlie Mortenson."

It happened. Like a sickness in my gut, I felt guilt rising. All the knowing buried inside me, a dark shadow clamouring to get out.

After my black-eye run in with Charlie Mortenson, I'd taken Auntie's advice and steered clear not only of the Mortensons, but most boys my age.

Instead, on weekends I'd stop by the small farm near the creek Frank Gilbert worked with his mum, and chat.

He wasn't like other grown-ups. He'd be at work, digging, his face perspiring and gleaming in the sunlight. But he was always happy to stop and pass the time of day. He'd tell me about any latest projects, proud of his most recent, a homemade billy-cart. But soon enough the Widow Gilbert would come out with a brow like a ploughed paddock.

"On your way, Frank's got work to do."

"Too right, work," Frank repeated, waving his spade as proof. His mother moved away to the chook yard.

"Swing by later," Frank whispered, "we'll race that billy-cart then."

And we did. Faces pink with the effort, faster and faster we pushed each other until we veered off the track in a storm of dust. Frank and me, we'd been laughing, wiping hands on our shirts, when the Widow came running out, mad as a cut snake.

"Frank, inside. *You! You* should know better," she yelled at me.

It was after that Frank's mother bailed up my aunt. Auntie Madge made me promise to stay away.

"But I like Frank. He's a mate."

"We're not our neighbours' mates or enemies either," she said. "Pull your head in is best."

Years later I worked it out; Widow Gilbert looked at me like all the rest. Another kid who'd claim to be her son's mate, then get older and tell his friends Frank was a dumb bloke with kangaroos loose in the top paddock. To her, I was another larrikin like Wayne Mortenson and, after him, his younger brother Charlie.

After the billy-cart business, walking along beside the creek one day I'd seen Charlie coming towards me. Dodging to one side, I squatted behind a bush.

"Hey, g'day," I heard.

I parted the branches and seeing his grin felt a sick jolt. But Charlie gestured to someone behind me, back up the hill.

"Frankie-boy, come squiz. Diamonds in the creek!"

Frank's voice came next. "Not supposed to talk to you," he said. "Mum says so."

Charlie shrugged, making as if to walk on.

"Shame," he said. "Still, reckon that diamond necklace will look bonzer on someone else's Ma."

"I love my Mum," Frank defended himself.

"Sure? Prove it."

I watched Frank pick his way down the hill towards where Charlie waited. A little distance still between them, Frank stopped. Charlie pointed.

"Diamonds, there!"

Frank took a step, stood squinting. When he bent forward, Charlie shoved, soaking him, and ran off. Frank left puzzled and dripping, I slipped away, ashamed.

But Charlie's hassling continued. Next time I was passing Frank's yard, I saw Charlie again. I ducked behind the chook shed.

"How goes it, Frankie," Charlie grinned.

Frank kept digging.

"Not talking," he said.

"Suit yourself. Means I can't give you a message, from a real pretty sheila," Charlie said. "Wants to meet you down at the creek."

I followed at a distance watching Frank wipe sweaty palms on his trousers.

"No girls," he said, looking about.

"Look!" Charlie pointed.

On a rock were some women's clothes, a dress, stockings, underwear. They looked like things worn by Charlie's Ma to me, but I guessed to Frank they were ladies' things, delicate, different to his mother's drab-coloured garments. From behind a bush on the other side of the creek a bare arm emerged and beckoned.

"Hey, Frankie. She wants to swim," Charlie said, "Get in, she's shy."

Frank undressed and, naked, waded into the water.

"Hello?" he called.

Wayne Mortenson crashed out of the bushes, crowing. A mate, rolling his sleeve down, followed.

"Have a geek at him," Wayne sneered.

"Strike me blue," his mate snorted.

It was Charlie who threw the first stone.

"Here, drongo!"

The others picked up more stones and threw. Frank raising his arms to hide his face, they all laughed harder. But soon enough Wayne and his mate stood back, saying they'd had enough. They strode away. Charlie, disappointed, trailed behind.

When he stopped close to where I was crouching, a pulse throbbed at my temple;

something between fear and anger. But Charlie's attention was on Frank.

He threw a parting shot, then another; stones big as he could hold.

I saw the last one skim off Frank's stomach. He smiled as if the jolt flicked a switch in his head, making the game easier to understand. Picking up a sizeable stone from the creek bed he stretched his muscular arm back as Charlie turned away. With all the strength of an adult man, he threw. The rock struck the back of Charlie's head with the loud crack of kindling breaking.

I stood, trembling.

"Charlie," Frank said, wading forward. His grin faded. "Wake up, Charlie."

The stillness of the bush closed in, tumbled around me into the full terror of meaning. I found Frank's eyes, frightened, fixed on mine. And that was the moment I turned, ran, long-legged in escape.

I heard after. They found Frank like that, sitting naked at the edge of the creek, cradling Charlie's bloodied head in his lap. No one understood what had happened. The Widow Gilbert insisted Frank had promised her he'd have nothing to do with those Mortensons. As for Frank, he didn't say a single word — about anything at all.

In the room next to the store cupboard Auntie Madge was pushing back her chair, standing up. The Widow Gilbert stood too.

"I'm sorry I can't help," Auntie Madge said, showing the Widow out.

"Will Widow Gilbert be coming back?" I asked.

"No point," Auntie Madge said. "Words that Widow wants, they're nothing I can give her."

The fog I felt inside darkened. Charlie Mortenson, gone. Frank Gilbert, not speaking. Even Auntie Madge's voices, silenced.

This time it was only me who could flash a light to unlock the words from beyond. I alone carried the match of a miracle.

Pomegranate

Anna Rachel

I'm through with him.
But the minute I say that,
pains course through me.
I can't bear to be rid
of that admirable outlet
that marvellous way
of making my mind
known to other people.

I have to ask myself;
would he take the time
to peel back the thin membranous flesh
to reveal delicious fruit?
No. He's too impulsive. Impatient.
Heavy handed. He'd crush
the fragile arils beneath
inconsiderate fingertips
Not on purpose
he doesn't know any better
It's second nature
Is it not?

We reach for the last one at the same time
I draw back
he turns to me, smiling wryly, "it's yours"
no it isn't
the second he knew he wanted it, it was his

I wave my hand,
giving him the permission he already had
I'm ready for the show
he tucks it under his arm
like fresh game
Only it isn't a limp duck
he looks lost

I can see it all in my head
him tossing it onto the counter
hacking into it with a knife
he thought it would be simple
he expected them to just pour out
waiting anxiously to be freed by him
he isn't the hero, and he can't work it out.

He's frustrated now
the arils beneath his thumbs
spraying juice on his face and chest
he chuckles at this retaliation
amused by pattern created on his white shirt
akin to blood spatter

The Track

George Graves

Despair.

The blackness seemed to soak through his very skin, trying to extinguish the small ember of brightness that still resided within him. He thought of it as though it was the warm glow of a small candle, not held particularly anywhere. Just somewhere. And now the glow, the hope, was beginning to flicker and fade.

He felt so silly. So ridiculous. Trying to walk back to his shack by the lake at this time of night. No moon. No stars — the layer of cloud had blocked them out. Oh, such a stupid thing to do. And he was cold. So cold. The thin shirt was not enough. Some extra clothes would have been a good idea. A pullover or a jacket, or both. But he had forgotten to take the warm coat when he had left.

It seemed such a simple thing to do. Just stroll along the track through the forest from her place down to the clearing that surrounded his home. Only a couple of miles. Somehow, he went off the track. He had walked that path many times. But now he had made a mistake along the way. It was easy to see why. It was not really a path. Just a narrow strip trodden down by him in the undergrowth, weaving between the trees and the scrubs and the rocks. Mostly it was fairly flat but there were a couple of steeper slopes which he needed to scramble up.

During the daytime, he loved this area. So quiet, with just the call of the birds. He, with some help from his "bird book", as he called it, could distinguish most of them now. Except for that crazy one that could mimic anything. Once he wondered who was cutting down trees in the forest with a chainsaw until he spotted the culprit. A drab looking, mid-grey bird, making such an incredible sound. Not a bird call at all but a crazy chainsaw noise.

He was lost. He knew that. And nobody would find him. Only one person knew he was somewhere out here, and she would assume he was back at his cabin, or shack as he called it, being a hermit again, only coming out to see her now and then or when he needed to collect some food at the village.

Well, I need to stop. Do I go to the left or the right? Or try turning around to head back? I'm not even sure which way back is. If I go any further, I may become even more lost, if that is possible. I have no idea where I am, but I can't be too far from the track. But which way is it?

I wonder if I can find some shelter? I may be lost now but I have wandered all over this area in the daytime. But I don't remember any caves nearby. I wouldn't be able to find them anyway.

What can I do? First, I need to reduce my heat loss. I don't really want to freeze to death out here. That would be rather a disappointment! What did I learn in that sailing survival course years ago? Tuck my knees up close to my chest and wrap your arms around them. What else can I do? If the wind gets up, find a hollow somewhere. Lean against a tree trunk so I am not wasting energy standing up. Might as well give it a go. Can't do any harm.

In the morning I can use the direction of the sunrise to walk towards the lake. Perhaps I'll meet the track, or else the foreshore. If I reach the lake, I probably would need to climb back up a bit to scout around that marshy area. And then to home!

Just need to survive tonight. I've stopped shivering now. That is not good.

I like my shack by the lake. It's so quiet and peaceful. I used to work so hard. Why was I preparing briefs late at night instead of going to those concerts Emma so loved attending? I don't know.

And then I found I simply could not push myself anymore. What was the use of it all? Couldn't stand all the noise and the bustle of the city. I must have been here for a couple of years now. Or is it a bit more? Not sure. Something like that.

There are no stars and the moon is not up yet. I'm really cold now.

Nicole must miss Phil so much. I really need to try to message her more often. What's her son's name? I keep on forgetting it. Yes. Alexander. That's it. He thinks the world of his old Pa. He told me that these messages I receive on the mobile are called SMS. I wonder if it is like fish. One fish and ten fish. Do we have one SMS and ten SMS or is it ten SMSs? Nicole seems to be coping ok but it must be so difficult for her after the car accident. I wonder how lonely she is?

Jeanne's great. I do enjoy being invited to her place. And the meal was wonderful. And she had beautiful music playing. Mozart and Brahms, symphonies and concertos. Must have a good battery out the back somewhere to run that CD player and those large speakers. Don't know what she sees in me. I'm not like I used to be. City just got too much, so came out to the shack. I enjoy being with her. She is friendly and witty and she has care and empathy. I guess, if I'm truthful, I'm scared of being with anyone now. Don't know why. But she's nice. I like her. Lots.

Was that a torch I saw flicker over there? Yes — there it is again. I must be about fifty yards off the track. Is she going to walk straight by? What can I do? Can't seem to yell. My voice doesn't seem to work. How can I make a noise? I know! I'll bash a tree with an old dead branch.

Yes. Yes. It worked. She's stopped. She's shining the torch this way — another bash — yes, I'm coming, I'm coming.

"There you are."

"Thank you. Thank you so much Jeanne. You found me."

"I'm having trouble understanding your slur, Richard. Here, I'll help you put on your jacket.

Your phone is still in the pocket. Your daughter sent you a message a while ago. Now, don't try to talk too much. We have to walk. Give me your arm. That's it, rest it on my shoulder and I'll put my arm around your waist. Ready? Is that a little nod? Yes. Good. Let's go. We're about half a mile from my cabin. We'll go there. It's closer.

"Really Richard. You must think about what you are doing. You seem to wander around with your mind somewhere else, like five million miles away in another universe. You've got to take notice of what you are doing. Even with a night like this you would have made it home if you had been thinking about looking for that track.

"You don't need to drop your head like that. I'll stop the lecture now.

"Was that a tiny chuckle I heard?

"And for an instant I saw that cheeky smile you have.

"Oh Richard. I was so worried I wouldn't find you.

"I'll keep on chatting on the way back to the cabin. You are probably wondering why I came out looking for you.

"You don't need to talk — I can see the nod. That's it. Keep on plodding along.

"Well, I woke up during the night, hours after you left, and saw your jacket still hanging by the door. I have never done this before but for some reason I had the feeling I needed to check that you had arrived safely back at your shack.

"Keep going — we are almost halfway now.

"So, I took your coat, hopped in the Jeep and zoomed up the track from my place, along the asphalt road and down that — whatever you call it — track to your place. Really, you need to have some of those potholes fixed. I almost got lost in one of them.

"It's nice to see that little smile.

"It's only about ten miles — didn't take too long.

"Well, you weren't there. So, you still had to be on the forest track between my place and yours.

"Got home, grabbed a torch from the Jeep and off I went. I'm glad you weren't too far along. It would have been a bit tricky getting you back down that rock scree if you had made it past that.

"You're going well — not too much further — we're past halfway home. See. There aren't so many shrubs now.

"I'll keep on rambling on. It might make the time seem less. What's that look mean? Do you think it may make the trip seem even longer? Naughty!

"You know, Richard, you are doing fairly well. Much better than you were when I met you a couple of years ago. Yes, I know the last fortnight has not been good. You don't need to tell me — I remembered it was the anniversary of the car accident.

"Oh, such sadness, Richard. For both of them as well as those who knew them. It would have been Emma's birthday last Monday also. She would have been about my age, wouldn't she.

"Not much now — I left the curtains open on this side of the house so we could see the glow through the window.

"It's ok to be sad. Appropriate actually. But you know it is not good for you to be a hermit all the time.

"Keep plodding. You're slowing down a bit.

"You do realise you would enjoy life a little more if you got out a little more. I know you love the view of the lake from your place, and the forest and all that, but you need to get out, and see people.

"How about, in a few weeks' time, we have dinner at the pub in the village. We don't need to stay for long — just a quick meal and leave. It would be good for me also.

"Was that a tiny nod? Thanks Richard.

"I'm chatting like — well I don't know what. I'm usually the quieter one, but I talk when I'm anxious.

"I'll flick the torch off for a moment. Look to the right, Richard. The trees have the faintest of shadows. We're just about there now — just around the bend and we'll be able to see the glow from the window.

"You're doing so well, Richard."

"We made it. We're here.

"Sit down at the table. No, not near the fire. You would warm up too quickly there.

"I'll put the kettle on. While it's boiling, I'll get those boots off you. Just stay put. It's ok.

"Quick cup of tea. There — now don't wobble your head so. It will be warm — not really hot the way you like it. I don't want you scalded on the inside as well as frozen on the outside. And some sugar. I know you don't usually have it but it may do you some good. Now, drink it slowly.

"And no alcohol."

"How do you know about this, Jeanne? Were you a nurse?"

"What was that? Wow, you really are slurring your words. I can hardly understand you. A nurse? Hopefully your memory will be better when you're over this. No. A primary school teacher. Don't get many cases of hypothermia in the dear little ones in a classroom. Well, I read about it some time ago. Now, strip off and get into my bed. You need to get warm slowly."

"But ... But."

"Just do as I say. Come on. I'll help you. I don't want your soggy socks or those wet jeans and shirt in my bed. That's it. No. No. You can leave those on.

"Here, I'll give you a hand to go to the bedroom. Off we go.

"Really Richard. Just jeans and a shirt. At this time of the year?

"You may be looking ahead but I can still see that expression.

"Yes. I'm nagging you — again. Aren't I? I'll stop now. Well, for a little while anyway. I like the smile. Now into bed.

"Right, I'll put another blanket on you. I'll also leave the lamp lit but turned down. I want to see if you change colour from that pasty white to someone who looks like they are living.

"Don't you cark it on me, Richard, you hear. The paperwork would be horrendous."

"I'll try … not to … Jeanne … I won't. I … promise."

"What? Good. Now from what I read I need to get you warm slowly. So, I'm getting into bed with you."

"Alright."

"But … what, what … are … you … doing?"

"What was that? Yea — I worked it out. What's it look like? I thought it would be obvious. I can't heat transfer, I think that was the term used in the article I read, to you if I have my coat and other things on."

"Oh, I … see. Alright … um … okay."

"This is purely for therapeutic reasons, you understand. That's all."

"That's all."

"Oh! Oh God! Oh! You're freezing! Oh!"

"Sorry."

"It's ok. Now just cuddle up to me. Oh my God! You are so cold.

"Oops, sorry again God. Yes, that's the way.

"Now put your arms around me. That's good. Just relax. Think of the time when we went hiking together alongside the lake and up that small creek. You thought of it and organised it. Thank you. I loved that time. And you loved it too, didn't you. Remember how cold the water was when we went swimming and how warm we were when we dried out on the bank on that sandy spot we found. It was so peaceful. The sun pouring down on us. The murmur of the leaves rustling from the slight breeze. That's it. Go to sleep now."

"Thanks … Jeanne … nite … nite."

"Goodnight, Richard."

I wonder if that kiss was purely for therapeutic reasons?

You Woman of Scraps

Kit Scriven

Someone told you they don't swoop
if you feed them. There's one you've named Father.
He swoops from the shadows. He loves your scraps.
He is an insinuator who sings dawn, dew,
you. His day job
involves negotiation with visitor or trespasser —
furies of sinew and feather. He works from home
and spends the quieter hours practising on family.

Along with morning and dew
Father sings seasons and sometimes frost
pearled
on fence wire —
images made for unfurling whenever he thinks
you might forget the white plumes
of your breath and his
colliding on walks to school. And how much
it matters.

The nest mentors black and white. You look up into
his face —
this being who made you and the contract,
the one about birth and allegiance and being
his.

Father inflects his song. Some days
you jump. Others
he pushes. Today
you fall. Today
he'll warble his dirge about the girl
who says she will not listen.

You woman of scraps. You fledgling, you woman of black.
You woman of white
plumes. You ruffle in the dirt
wanting
and not wanting the ranger.

You woman of scraps. You worshipper
of light pearled on fence wire. You worshipper
of fight nested beyond the ranger. You worshipper
of flight
swooping beyond birth and allegiance

into being.

CONTRIBUTORS

The Alice Sinclair Memorial Writing Competition is run biannually by the Lake Macquarie Branch of the Fellowship of Australian Writers, NSW — abbreviated as Lake Macquarie FAW.

Coming out of the shadows are the following contributors who submitted those stories and poems considered by the judges in 2022 to be the best.

POETRY CONTRIBUTORS

First prize: *Janice Williams*
Second prize: *Kathryn Fry*
Highly commended: *Gideon McDonald*

Agi Dobson, *Epiphany*

Agi arrived in Australia, aged eight, from Hungary, so English is her second language. She became hooked on writing poetry when in Year 7 she was introduced to Shakespeare and the classic English poets. As a result, much of Agi's poetry is emotionally charged. She used lockdown to put together her first poetry collection, titled *Feelings* … published last year by Stringybark Press.

Agi has written two commissioned school textbooks, worked as a journalist and in publicity. She has written a feature length film script, which won a Commendation in the Fellowship of Australian Writers' scriptwriting competition and keeps searching for an interested producer. However, her main passion remains poetry. Agi is regularly published in a number of small press magazines.

Having recently moved to the green hills of South Gippsland, the landscape inspires her writing and has motivated her to dabble in painting.

Amy Purton-Long, ***Night Feathers (forgive me)***

Amy has been writing for as long as she can remember, with early success in poetry competitions and slams around Brisbane. Amy went on to work briefly in screenwriting, where she was surprised to find herself editing a TV show about teen mermaids, before a foray into feature journalism. After a long break from poetry Amy has returned to this beloved form, through which she can express her love, curiosity and sometimes sadness for all the beautiful, fragile things on this planet we call home.

David Kelly, ***Ashmore Prophets***

David believes that writing a poem is like building a stone wall; just picking up the next stone is not good enough. You have to give in to the synchronicity of mind and rock, juggle the stony words until they look good, sound good, feel good: until they fall into the pattern they had in mind and they tell you what you wanted to say.

David's concrete poetry book, called *BOOK*, was published with Eaglemont Press in 2000. His first conventional poetry book, *planes, birds, cats, things* was published with Ginninderra Press in 2021 and a second, *The handyman and other poems,* is scheduled for early 2023. To paraphrase Shakespeare: the poem's the thing!

Gideon McDonald, *Between the Speckled Lights*

Gideon is 29 years old and lives in Fremantle (Walyalup), Whadjuk land, Western Australia. He works at a bookstore (New Edition), having studied for a Bachelor of Ancient History (UWA).

He completed his Honours degree at University of Western Australia in Literary Studies which focused on the philosophy of Nikos Kazantzakis in his novel *Zorba the Greek*.

Ian Reid, *The Great Seal*

Ian's poems have appeared in many Australian magazines and anthologies, as well as overseas. Book-length selections of his poetry have been published in Australia, Canada and the USA, and translated into Korean.

He is the author of five novels, the most recent of which, *The Madwoman's Coat*, 2021, was longlisted for the ARA Historical Fiction Prize. His international awards include the Antipodes prize for poetry.

Ian has been a director of the Australian Society of Authors, a peer reviewer for the Australia Council, and a judge of the WA Premier's Literary Awards.

His poem 'The Great Seal' refers to an enigmatic oil painting of that name by the notable Perth artist Ben Joel, which has adorned the wall of Ian's home for more than 30 years.

Irina Frolova, ***To the Sun***

Irina is a Russian-Australian writer. She has a degree in philology from Moscow City Pedagogical University and is studying psychology at Deakin University. She is a member of several writing communities and the current President of the Lake Macquarie FAW. Her work speaks to the experience of immigration, neurodivergence, and a search for belonging. It draws on folklore and explores archetypes through cultural and feminist lenses.

Her poetry and prose have appeared in *Not Very Quiet*, the *Australian Poetry Collaboration, Baby Teeth Journal, Rochford Street Review, The Blue Nib, The Australian Multilingual Writing Project, Live Encounters, Mascara Literary Review, Kalliope X*, and *Burrow*. Her creative highlights include her first collection of poetry, *Far and Wild* (released by Flying Island Books in 2021), and winning the second prize in the 2021 Deborah Cass Prize for writing. You can find Irina on Facebook @irinafrolovapoet

Janice Williams, ***Boy with a Trumpet***

Janice has been writing most of her life. Fortunately, early attempts no longer exist. She is president of her local writers' group, edits her church's newspaper, and belongs to two Society of Women Writers Victoria email workshop groups. She finds competitions a great way to hone her writing skills. She has self-published two books, *Stir of Wings* and *Times and Seasons,* and been involved in joint publication of a third, *Let the Sea Roar*. She is an optometrist, now retired – leaving more time for writing!

The poem 'Boy with a Trumpet' refers to 'Wake up the Dawn' in 2020, when COVID-19 forced cancellation of Anzac ceremonies. Twelve-year-old Jack stands playing the Last Post on his trumpet, his three siblings lighting the darkness with candles. It speaks of children a century earlier, whose fathers and older brothers never returned.

J. Marahuyo, *Winter High*

J. Marahuyo is a Filipino-Australian poet currently residing on Wangal country. Her poems have placed in a number of competitions, and she has work in *Cordite Poetry Review,* and the *Living Stories Things Unsaid* anthology. She was shortlisted for the inaugural Born Writer's Award. Her work can be found on their website as well as in *ZineWest* and the *Short Stories Unlimited Seasons* anthology.

She was selected to take part in the following mentorship programs for 2022: WestWords Academy, Express Media's Toolkits Lite: Poetry & The Writing Zone.

She explores themes of identity, mental health and everyday moments as whimsically as possible and is currently working on her first collection of poetry.

Her Instagram is @j_marahuyo

Kate Maxwell, *Let There be a Firmament*

Kate is a teacher and writer from Sydney. She's been published and awarded in many Australian and International literary magazines. Her first poetry anthology, *Never Good at Maths* (IP Press) was published in 2021, and her second anthology is forthcoming in 2023. Kate enjoys writing in many genres including speculative fiction, flash, YA, and poetry. Her interests include film, wine, and sleeping.

Kathryn Fry, *Antidote* and *The Old Sand Mining Site*

Kathryn moved to Belmont eleven years ago, and since then, has enjoyed being a member of the Hunter Writers Centre (HWC) and Eastlakes U3A. For eight and five years respectively she co-ordinated a HWC poetry group and the Creative Writing class of U3A.

Her poems have been published in *Antipodes* (2016, 2019), *Cordite Poetry Review* (2016), *Not Very Quiet* (2017-2020 inclusive), *Westerly* (2019, 2020) and *Science Write Now* (2020-2022 inclusive). In 2020, her poem 'About the Centre, Even Now' won the Alice Sinclair competition poetry category, and she was longlisted for the ACU

Prize for Poetry. Her first collection is *Green Point Bearings* (2018) and her second *The Earth Will Outshine Us* (2021) – both through Ginninderra Press.

Kit Scriven, *You Woman of Scraps*

Kit writes short stories and poems with a rural flavour. He has won or been shortlisted in several short story competitions. 'You woman of scraps' is the first time one of his poems has been shortlisted. Kit's current focus is on *The plains-wanderer,* a literary novel set on the irrigation plains of northern Victoria.

The inspiration for 'You woman of scraps' came from watching a neighbour feeding a magpie she had befriended. It inspired Kit to contemplate the complications of family relationships and how difficult it is to navigate through life.

Pippa Kay, *Miasma*

Pippa is an award-winning short story writer, now trying her hand at poetry. She experiments with ekphrastic challenges posted on Rattle.com each month and 'Miasma' was inspired by one of these.

Pippa is a member of The Fellowship of Australian Writers (Isolated Writers), Writing NSW, and The Society of Women Writers where she coordinates workshops. Some decades ago she taught Creative Writing to adults and a small group from those classes now meet weekly at each other's houses to discuss and critique their writing.

She has been successful in many short story competitions and her collected stories titled *Keeping it in the Family*, published by Ginninderra Press, won the Society of Women Writers Fiction Prize in 2018.

More information at: www.pippakay.com.au

Rees Campbell, *Eleven Steps*

Rees is Tasmanian by birth and attitude. She is passionate about the island she was lucky enough to be born on; its extraordinary places, creatures, plants and people which inspire her writing. Love and place – for Rees there cannot be one without the other. Islandness is paramount. She writes about her loves, the joys and losses.

Whilst poetry is her focus, Rees is known for her nonfiction works about Tasmanian shore life, and the edible native plants. Her poetry and short stories have been published in numerous anthologies; and she has written six books, the most recent being *Eat MORE Wild Tasmanian*.

Her inspiration for 'Eleven Steps' was her son, who was a nurse in Melbourne during the covid dark times.

SHORT STORY CONTRIBUTORS

First prize: *Marc Cannella*
Second prize: *Ned Stephenson*
Highly commended: *Edith Speers* & *Roslyn Varley*

Allan Nicholls, *The Sign*

Allan started writing many years ago, but when the first publisher sent back his first rejection notice, he put his book in a box and forgot about it. In 2011 after a medical challenge, Allan re-wrote it and the book has now been published.

Allan lives in Lake Macquarie and is a member of the Australian Christian Writers' Fellowship. Allan wrote this story because of the dreadful manner in which veterans were treated by the public, the media and the government, on returning from the Vietnam war.

Anne Andrews, *Grandad*

Anne has, after 57 years teaching in PNG and Australia, decided to devote herself to her lifelong passion of creative writing. She has won several prizes for poetry, short stories and photography and her other creative outlet is landscape gardening, which she indulges with her artist husband John. Her creative efforts have been published in *New England Country Living,*

New England Living, High Lean Country (book edited by Alan Atkinson), FAWQ magazine *Scope,* NZ Writers *College Times, ROAM* magazine and the FAW anthology *Much More Than Words.*

To raise funds for Rotary's Polio Plus campaign, Anne self-published three booklets of her poems – titled *Atmospheric, Comic* and *Magic,* and is currently planning her fourth book of poems. She dreams of one day publishing a novel set in the steamy jungles of Papua New Guinea, and a series of novellas of a Miss Marple type unravelling cold cases in rural NSW.

Black Crow Walking, *Rapunzel and the Awakening*

Crow has trained and worked as a professional artist since her children grew up 20 years ago. She followed in her father's footsteps as an artist and eventually was a forerunner in painting with encaustic and cold wax in Australia. Since losing the use of her studio, she has turned her artistic talent to writing.

She has two self-published books of poetry called *Drifting Leaves* and *Captured Moments,* published in 2019. The same year she also published her first non-fiction book, *Angels Speak*. Since then, she has been in two anthologies, *Sapphic Touch* and *Sapphic Flows* and two for Poetry in the Pub. She is currently writing a nonfiction encyclopedia about spirituality and, for light relief, is rewriting Grimm's fairy tales. Her story of Rapunzel, which appears in this anthology, is one of those tales.

Bronwyn MacRitchie, *Break In*

Bronwyn has been writing short stories since childhood. Upon retirement from music teaching, she began attending workshops with an interest in creative writing and memoir. In 2020, she published *Pixie Dust*, a memoir of her childhood and in 2021, during Covid lockdown, produced an audio version of her book.

She is a member of both Hunter Writers and Lake Macquarie FAW and has been a frequent finalist in the Newcastle Herald Short Story Competition. Bronwyn is currently working on her next memoir.

Christine Johnson, *Words from Beyond*

Christine is an emerging writer who lives on the Central Coast, NSW, with her partner and their rescue Cavoodle, Meg. After a career in Australia and Hong Kong as a professional theatre director, she returned to writing (a lifelong passion).

Her short stories have won awards and appear in numerous anthologies. Her stories have been shortlisted for the 2017 Alan Marshall

Short Story Award, the 2018 Elyne Mitchell Writing Awards, and the 2019 Stuart Hadow Prize. In 2019 she also won first prize in the inaugural Sydney Hammond Memorial Writing Competition. Second prizewinner in the 2020 Port Stephens Literature Award, she was published in Newcastle Short Story Award 2022.

In 2014, her first novel manuscript attracted funding from Accessible Arts, NSW, allowing her to work with a professional editor. After redrafting, it won first place in the 2019 Eggcellent Manuscript Assessment Competition and, in 2021, was longlisted in the Hawkeye Publishing Manuscript Development Prize. A hardworking optimist, Christine intends to improve her novel towards publication and is currently working on her second.

Edith Speers, *The Flying Fortuna Sister*

Edith was born in Canada, grew up in Vancouver, and completed a Bachelor of Science (Hon. Biochem.) at Simon Fraser University then emigrated to Australia where her poetry and short stories have won many literary awards.

Her work has been published in all the major Australian literary magazines and many anthologies, as well as several Canadian and American journals.

She is the author of three published collections of poetry. She has also published other Australian writers as proprietor of Esperance Press.

'The Flying Fortuna Sister' is one of a series of stories that she wrote which all start with 'Once upon a time'. This phrase, usually confined to children's stories, sends immediate signals: something magical will happen; you will suspend disbelief as children do; and embedded in the events there will be a lesson. In this case, the inspiration was a friend who said, 'I was so happy I was floating around the house'.

George Graves, *The Track*

George has been a member of the Lake Macquarie FAW for about ten years, writing short stories and some poems, mostly about people and relationships. Although they are largely fictional, he often draws on incidents from his past and incorporates these into the stories.

George has a mathematics and electronic engineering background, so these have a very different style from that used in engineering journals where his name has appeared amongst the authors of various papers.

He loves reading about many different topics, including mathematics and quantum physics, but also often reads novels. George owns an old yacht and enjoys messing about in it on Lake Macquarie, where all the trivia of this world seems to fade away. He is particularly thankful for the encouragement he has received from members of the writing group to which he belongs.

Gurgica Georgina Chakar, *Levisia*

Georgina's story-telling talent was first recognised in her high school years. Her work was inspired by her inner perception of the world, translated into creative literary works through the real people and events around her.

Her first published works were children's plays for radio adaptation. While working on writing, editing, and publishing her first novel, Georgina has written several short stories, one of which has been shortlisted by the Alice Sinclair competition.

Residing in the Emirates for over a decade, Georgina wrote several professional articles in the eminent *Middle East Architect* magazine, a publication distributed across the Middle East. Collaboration with the magazine spanned several years. Georgina is also a painter of abstract works. She lives and works in Sydney.

Kim Michelle Ross, *Reckoning*

Kim started writing full-time in 2005, studying Creative Writing and Writing for Publication at the Hunter WEA College 2005-06. She joined the Hunter Writers' Centre in 2007 and facilitated Women@theLockup writers in 2009.

She won a LitLink Mentorship in 2010, with multi-award-winning speculative-fiction author and poet, Jenny Blackford. Her debut novel *Netherrealm, Book 1: Heed the Darkness* won a Silver Recommended Read Badge, 2019 Author Shout Ready Reader Awards, an Honourable Mention and Silver 5-Star Review badge, Readers' Favorite 2020 International Book Awards, and Quarterfinalist 2022 ScreenCraft Cinematic to Book Competition.

In 2013 through NaNoWriMo she completed a paranormal rom-com title: *Death*: *It's Complicated* which, though unpublished, received a 5-Star review medal and 2022 Readers Favorite International Book Awards. She has 19 short stories published in 15 anthologies, web journals and e-zines.

Being alone and feeling creeped-out in the Lockup while hearing the outside world was Kim's inspiration for writing 'Reckoning'.

Kylie Moppert, *Not Like Him*

Kylie is fortunate that, when she picks up an interest, she often becomes obsessed by it. During Covid-19, while running her artisan bakery, she started taking online creative writing courses. Running her micro artisan bakery had been an all-consuming passion but writing quickly took precedence. In June 2022 she sold her bakery for a sabbatical of writing.

Kylie is delighted that 'Not Like Him' is her first shortlisted story. The idea came from exploring the 'origin scene' (an experience which teaches a character a lesson they must later unlearn).

The story underwent several iterations before reaching the version submitted to the Alice Sinclair competition for the *Out of the Shadows* anthology. Constant, though, was the rooming house in St Kilda, and the young teenager who needs to see their estranged, traumatised father.

Marc Cannella, *Distant Fires*

Marc has been writing both nonfiction and fiction for a number of years, and his interest in period settings, classic literature, history and character-driven stories seemed well suited to the topic of this anthology, *Out Of The Shadows*.

After studying Professional Writing and Editing at Victoria University TAFE, he has mostly been published in the realm of television and movie reviews, as well as motor racing and Aussie Rules football.

He has a love of the English language, words in general and short-form writing, and despite periods of inactivity, seems to rely on bursts of inspiration to quench his creative thirst.

Marie Heitz, *The Short Story*

Marie is a practising doctor in Hobart whose writing seems fated for 'roundaboutedness'. She always intended to write, but only got there in her late 50s after practicing various forms of medicine all over the place.

In 2021 her lumpy bolted-together first novel left home to seek its fortune amongst agents and publishers, accumulating the rejections which are the lot of ugly unformed things. Then an unsuspecting editor with her submissions drawbridge raised was caught unawares by a chance email and *The Diemen Alexander* slipped into Fortress Clan Destine Press. He is due out, shaped and burnished, in February 2023.

'The Short Story' was first about a vampire who wasn't, but at 1500 words, the vampire hadn't appeared, so it became the first chapter of a novel. By 2,000 words, it looked like the chapter itself could work as a short story, just Out of the Shadows from another angle.

Ned Stephenson, *Son of Prometheus*

Ned found the courage to begin penning tales when his first entry into a writing competition was selected for the Hunter Writers' Centre Short Story anthology of 2019.

Since then, he has written three books and has his mind set on at least a dozen more. All he needs to do is lose his phone and keep the cat off his keyboard. www.nedstephenson.com

Peter Court, *Mouse Tail*

Peter was born in a psychiatric hospital in Scotland and was then carried to Australia where he has settled in very nicely. He has produced and hosted breakfast and drive time radio shows whilst writing TV satire, magazine editorials and working as a regular newspaper columnist.

He has degrees in Psychology, Media, and a PhD in Creative Writing, which he now teaches at university. He has four beloved children who have all made it to wise adulthood.

Roslyn Varley, *Ghosts*

Ros can be found scribbling away in the cafes and libraries of Melbourne/Naarm. She writes short stories and plays. 'Ghosts' celebrates her mum, long gone now, and the sharing of endless card games with her at the kitchen table of the old farmhouse in central New South Wales. Mum's pithy personality and quirky turns of phrase are there in the story; also something of her response to the challenges and beauty of rural life. The darker side of 'Ghosts' is largely imagined, seeking to highlight the legacy of Australia's early settler society and its brutal impact on the Indigenous people of this country.

Sarah Bennett, ***The Parts that Hurt***

Sarah has a Bachelor of Arts in Writing and English. She writes about moments that might otherwise go unnoticed and explores their beauty through poetry and short stories. She is inspired most by everyday life: what is considered ordinary, what doesn't shout for attention.

She began writing as a teenager to challenge herself to be more creative, and soon found she didn't want to do anything else.

One day she hopes to publish a novel, but until then you can read her weekly posts on her blog, thesoftestwords.com

Sinead Reilly, ***R&R***

Sinead is a writer and editor who at the age of fourteen moved to Broken Hill, NSW, where the stark landscapes (paired with the influence of Steinbeck and McCarthy) spurred her to begin writing.

Her work has thus far centred around obsession, remorse, and paranoia, and she now finds much inspiration in the works of Faulkner as well as film directors including Kenneth Lonergan and Steve McQueen.

Sinead's short-listed entry was not brainstormed or thought out, but came to her entirely on a whim.

Tom Williamson, *The Old Time Swing*

Tom is a writer who is completing an Engineering and Arts (English) double degree for his undergraduate studies. Tom has written since he was a teenager and loves exploring genres of fantasy, and contemporary fiction.

This is Tom's first entry for the Alice Sinclair competition, where a story revolving around vivid flashbacks in a retirement home unearths the themes of Out of the Shadows.

Tom is also working on an anthology of short stories for his university which is more heavily centred around high-fantasy and magical systems. Tom likes to write from a background of research, where ideas stem from real world events, mythology, or key aspects of previous eras.

He loves using competitions and anthologies as a method to improve his writing with the help of professionals and world-class readers.

EDITING TEAM CONTRIBUTORS

Alison Ferguson

Alison is one of the editors of this anthology. Since retiring from work as a speech pathologist in clinical and academic settings, Alison has written a number of prize-winning short stories in crime, horror, and science fiction. She self-published *The Sisters' Saga* (a historical fiction trilogy) in 2021. Her science-fiction novel *Grey Nomad* was recently published under the imprint of Brio Books.

Pam Garfoot

Pam Garfoot is a writer, illustrator and artist. She is passionate about many aspects of the creative life and Australian pioneer history. Her first book *Making Them Real: Finding a Queensland Past* was co-authored with her sister, Elizabeth Conway, and won the Queensland Family History Society's Book Award for 2014. She has also written several journal articles, travel articles, and book reviews. Some of her short stories and poems have been published and have received commendations.

In 2020 Pam produced the illustrations for the first anthology published by Lake Macquarie writers, *Beneath the Surface*. Pam's second co-authored book, *Capricorn Drover*, was published in February 2023. Having moved away from Canberra ten years ago, after a long career in government libraries and in information management, she now lives on the shores of Lake Macquarie, New South Wales.

Sandra Joy

Sandra Joy recently supervised the Alice Sinclair Memorial Writing Competition. Since 2020, she has published nine books - a nonfiction book on helping others; *Life: a variant of adventure* (an anthology of her short stories); and seven children's *Happy Helper* books – all while studying a Bachelor of Arts.

www.ingramcontent.com/pod-product-compliance
Lightning Source LLC
Chambersburg PA
CBHW061056100726
47911CB00012B/262

* 9 7 8 0 9 0 9 4 9 7 9 0 3 *